Management Strategies for WOMEN

or, NOW THAT I'M BOSS, HOW DO I RUN THIS PLACE?

Ann McKay Thompson & Marcia Donnan Wood

 Simon and Schuster / NEW YORK

Copyright © 1980 by Ann McKay Thompson and Marcia Donnan Wood
All rights reserved
including the right of reproduction
in whole or in part in any form
Published by Simon and Schuster
A Division of Gulf & Western Corporation
Simon & Schuster Building
Rockefeller Center
1230 Avenue of the Americas
New York, New York 10020

SIMON AND SCHUSTER and colophon are trademarks of
Simon & Schuster
Designed by Irving Perkins Associates

Manufactured in the United States of America
10 9 8 7 6 5 4 3 2 1

Library of Congress Cataloging in Publication Data

Thompson, Ann McKay.
Management strategies for women.

Includes index.
    1. Women executives.   2.   Management.   I.   Wood,
    Marcia Donnan, joint author.   II.   Title.
HF5500.2.T56   658'.0088042   80-20752
ISBN 0-671-25476-6

Acknowledgments

WE GRATEFULLY acknowledge our "bandwagon builders" for their support and valuable contributions: Margaret Adams, Cristine Candela, Mary King, Patricia S. Lindh, Audrey Rowe, Patricia Schroeder, Joy Simsonson, Julia M. Walsh, and Ruth Whitney.

Also, our deepest appreciation to Stuart Madnick, John (Jack) Rockart, and Jeff Meldman, who provided excellent technical information for our planning and computer chapters.

Our thanks also to the South Dakota State Library, especially to M. J. Dustin for her superb research assistance, to Beth Christie, who marvelously struggled through our handwritten notes, and to the many, many managers and executives who confidentially shared with us their secrets of success, their fears, and their wishes for the future.

Personal and heartfelt thanks to Beulah and Larry McKay, Lois and Walter Thompson, Patricia Owens, Krissy and Alan Donnan, Ben and Delphine Hawkins—for reasons they each will understand.

Finally, we give a special acknowledgment to our loyal Katie, Katherine C. Owesney, for her encouragement and outstanding technical and professional assistance.

To Charlie and Charles
for their patience, wisdom, and support

Contents

9

Contents

Contents

CONTENTS

Contents

Introduction

THIS IS a book of dynamic strategies, self-tests, helpful lists, exercises, interviews, and humor. It is designed to help working women assess their organizations, their own jobs, their performances, their progress in their careers, and, finally, their general business know-how. Further, it is intended to help women learn more about organizations and processes, to understand where they fit into it all, and to develop management strategies for themselves and their organizations.

Management Strategies for Women deals with the substance of work, and includes some of the most common but least-written-about problems and opportunities in management. It is intended to be an exercise in management and an exploration of situations a woman may not experience until she is in the driver's seat. We hope that it also provides some solutions to problems, as well as lighter moments to brighten life in the fast-paced management world.

The book demands a great deal of the reader. It asks for introspection and inspection, for analysis and decisions, for *involvement.* It should be explained at the outset that this is not a management text for women executives. It is, instead, a how-to exercise based on sound management principles, common sense, and a lot of executive experience—ours and that of dozens of other managers with whom we have been associated. We also have used information gained through research, formal management courses, and extensive interviews with executives across the country to develop this unique book on practical management.

We also think it is important to explain at the outset that information in this book is not based on success stories alone. Indeed, one learns as much—and sometimes more—from a negative management experience as one does from a positive experience. And surely one suffers more from the negative!

The need for this book seemed to us to be many-faceted. First of all, we believe that women in the business world have entered a new phase. Lessons on assertiveness, basic rules for success, how to dress, managing career and home, and similar advice are simply not enough for the new woman manager. She needs to know more about her own abilities and interests and how they fit or do not fit into her job. She needs to be able to assess her job, her skills, her potential. She needs information that helps her learn more about the workings of an organization and how she can function most effectively within it.

Through our contact with American women in workshops we conducted, courses we attended, business sessions in which we engaged, we kept hearing the wish for information that presented common working-world situations and problems. Women wanted a tool to allow them to *experience* aspects of management, one that would allow them to make decisions about self and strategies. It wouldn't hurt, either, if there were a chance to try some "practice shots" to stimulate thinking or promote honesty with oneself about personal work issues.

And, although much has been written and said about the subjects, we heard the strong desire for further discussion about male/female working relationships and tokenism.

Secondly, we knew firsthand about the frustrations of daily management activity, about political bombs thrown in the way of female managers, about mistakes that can be made because practice and theory may differ. We knew about the occasional need for humor. And we knew the joys of management when everything was going according to strategy or was going well in spite of a plan.

Our positions in government, small business, education, journalism, and national corporate life put us in close contact with many other soldiers in the same managerial trenches we had been occupying. We were able to observe both female and male managers' reactions to self, situations, and systems. And we believed it was time to talk about it all.

Some words about style and format: The style here is informal and conversational—by design. We think it is more like the discussions managers often like to have with each other, one that allows for a personal kind of exchange.

Deciding on format was not difficult for us. We wanted to present information in a fairly concise manner that could facilitate easy reference. In addition, we liked the idea of different visual displays rather than the standard narrative format one might expect.

We risked including self-tests and quizzes in our discussions because we believed they would be helpful and sometimes entertaining. We say "risked" because there are those who contend that exposing women to self-testing can have a negative impact on them if they do not measure up. Also, the exercises were not designed by professional testers or psychologists, although a Ph.D. psychologist *was* consulted and one of us had extensive training and experience in tests and measurements. We felt the risks were worth it.

We sincerely hope that the risks involved for *you* in opening yourself up to the suggestions made in *Management Strategies for Women* will help you to make sound decisions about yourself and your organization.

1. What to Expect the First Few Months in a New Management Job

GOING INTO a new management job can be exhilarating. It means new challenges, opportunities, and possibilities. It may mean increased salary potential and significant career advancement. The new job might be the one position you have been waiting for, the one that will allow you to use your talents as never before. Surely there will be new doors opening, new contacts to make.

What happens after you unpack your briefcase and move in may not be as exhilarating. It may be downright discouraging, especially if one is unaware of the kinds of problems that often confront a new manager. Even experienced managers—whether male or female—face problems, fears, and frustrations common to the new-boss-in-the-building syndrome.

What we find amazing is that this transition period is rarely discussed. What new manager wants others to know she is not in total control right from the start? And, because it's *not* discussed very often, we have discovered that many new managers go through a rather miserable period wondering what they've gotten themselves into and not realizing that the period *is* transitory and that, believe it or not, things get better in a hurry.

"Why didn't someone tell me it would be like this?" several managers who survived the process asked us. And this is why we decided to try.

The following is a montage of observations, summaries, and quotes on a variety of topics related to moving into a new job. They are presented in this rather unorthodox style to help readers experience the *feelings* of others.

FRUSTRATION AND PANIC

• "The barrage of information is unbelievable. My desk was piled high with papers and reports. I was too new to sort out the important from the less important, much less answer the horde of letters asking for help or a decision. In many cases, I had no idea to whom the letters should be forwarded for assistance in responding. I simply could not find enough hours in the day to handle the paperwork, let alone find time to meet the staff and deal with substantive issues." • "Continuous interruptions by staff and outsiders became frustrating to me." • Some managers enter a broadly defined job where responsibilities and authority are not made clear. "I spent a week just trying to figure out what the job was all about. I thought I knew before I went into it, but in reality there seemed so much to do that I didn't know where to begin. I wasn't sure I'd be right if I *did* do something!" • "I felt frustrated and forever in a dilemma. No matter which way I wanted to go, there were 'Catch-22s,' no black and white. Sometimes I felt it was better not to make a decision and just let the inertia of the organization carry a problem to some unplanned solution." • A feeling of panic occurred among leaders who believed that everyone was counting on them to provide immediate, inspired leadership. It soon passed when they realized it was "absurd to think I have to know and do *everything.*"

SUBORDINATES VYING FOR SUPPORT

• During the first few weeks, a manager may be asked to attend meetings of her staff where she finds herself pressured to support a subordinate and his position before she is ready to do so. No advance warning of the pressure tactic is given. • "Staff members on the opposite side of an issue kept asking me to lunch in order to get an inside track. They were using the lunch game as a means of competing—against each other and for my attention."

FORCING RELATIONSHIPS

• "People are either with you or they're not. It's up to them. You can do everything you can to bring them on board, but in the end, it has to be their choice. Trying to force them backfires." • "I had to keep remembering that I was there to lead—not to be loved by everybody. I couldn't *make* them like me."

LOOKING FOR RATS AND SNAKES

• "There are always people in an organization who have an axe to grind. It comes out as they form secret coalitions to protect their interests, try to get a manager to reverse an unpopular decision made prior to her arrival, drop hints about getting rid of someone they don't like, or generally complain about previous management." New managers need to be aware of these individuals. However, some neophytes get so caught up in the paranoia of wondering who is out to get them that they have trouble trusting anyone for a long time. They find themselves immobilized. • "I was astounded when this male supervisor came to me and said he had been an unsuccessful candidate for my job and that he intended to have it, someday. He really threw me off balance." A number of managers have experienced this designed-to-make-her-paranoid play.

WHEN TO SAY, "I DON'T KNOW"

• "I guess everyone hates to admit she doesn't know something about the organization she heads. It's really tempting to pretend you are familiar with an area so your staff thinks you are exceptionally qualified to be the boss." • "Until I know the players, I have trouble leveling with them about things I don't know or don't have an answer for." • "I didn't feel I had a strong enough background in the area I was to supervise. But I banked on my management skills to overcome my lack of knowledge about the business. However, I expected some pretty tough challenges on what I did or did not know. It doesn't happen that much. Challenges related mainly to how I was going to *manage* the place." • "Women are too accustomed to being accommodating. It's easy for many of us to feel forced into making a decision. I had to stop being that way. I had to insist on being given enough time to make responsible decisions."

INSECURITIES

• "Will these new responsibilities mean I'm going to have to make some sacrifices that will ruin my personal life?" "Is this job going to pay enough to make it worthwhile?" "Will my friends think I've gone high-hat now that I'm in this position?" • "I was insecure about going outside the organization where I was expected to be an authority on something in the business which was very complicated. The crash course by my staff helped, but I was shaky on really technical questions." • "If I made tough personnel or administrative decisions, would the boss or board really stand behind me as they had promised to do?" "Could I really kick people out of the organization who should be sent packing? Could I handle the pressure from the community and their peers if I did?" • "It was frightening to have no knowledge about the power bases, because it's easier to calculate risks when you know where the power is. You can get hit from your blind side and may not be able to cope if you don't have the power bases identified." • Some new managers had a real concern about their ability to supervise. "I knew I was an expert in the industry but I'd never supervised many people before. I had to keep building my own confidence that I'd make good decisions and that, with some study, the management of people would follow." • Others wondered about their desire to manage people. "I'm not certain I really will enjoy being the boss. Maybe I won't like all of that responsibility. Maybe I won't be able to live with the day-to-day business of managing people."

DEALING WITH NEW POWER AND INFLUENCE

• "I was too much in awe of higher-ups and hadn't brought myself up to the level where I could deal comfortably with them. It took about a month for me to overcome it. The awe was eroded as I had more contact with them." • "I wondered if I was intelligent enough to make decisions that affected many segments of the population. I realized that I'd have to be very careful about how I used my power, and I quit being intimidated by others whom I assumed were brighter than I just because of their titles or professions." • "It takes a while to realize the influence and power you have. You learn it as you make demands on staff time and they are met, propose a budget change and it happens, map out a course and it's followed, make an off-the-cuff statement and it winds up becoming policy or a newspaper headline. . . . I guess I would recommend laying off the off-the-cuff statements for a while!"

INITIAL WORRIES ABOUT STAFF

• Acceptance and respect were at the head of the list. "Would the staff play games with me?" "Will individuals circumvent my position and go to others higher up or outside the organization?" • Sabotage was an issue. "I found my staff keeping back information from me because they did not want me to succeed. In an effort to eliminate my new job, they let me get in hot water and extremely embarrassing situations. After I finally caught on, I started asking them, 'Is there anything I need to know that you haven't had a chance to tell me?' Amazing how they changed when I held them responsible for getting information to me." • Loyalty was the next most prevalent concern. "In this organization, people are like vampires when there's a change in management. Loyalty is up for grabs." "I worried a great deal about whether people could shift their loyalty from the past boss to me. It made me wonder how far I could go in asking assistants to help me without their telling everyone I wasn't running the show."

FIRST STAFF MEETINGS

• The larger the staff, the more frequently managers wanted to postpone their first full staff meetings until they had met all key individuals on a one-to-one basis. Most leaders wanted to avoid the posturing, rhetoric, and negative group dynamics that are possible in a large meeting. They felt individuals would be more honest if they didn't initially have to express their opinions in front of their peers or in a group. • Other anxieties managers experienced were related to "being on display," "making a good first impression," "projecting myself as a leader and having the staff perceive me as such," "being able to run an effective meeting," and "feeling as if I were in competition with the previous manager, who did a great job."

PROBLEMS WITH THE BOSS

• "I had a lot of questions, but I didn't want to be a pest or make her think I couldn't figure things out." • "My boss was so powerful that it was difficult to assert myself. It made me feel that I was in training for at least two months until I got people coming to me about things *I* should handle rather than going to him." • "My position had been vacant for a while, so the job duties were farmed out to several managers. I had trouble collecting them; some people were reluctant to let go. I also had trouble getting the boss to quit making decisions I should be making. He knew he could make them much faster and was not willing, at first, to allow the extra time I required to study the problem and make a decision." • "When I finally arrived on the scene, the boss was so delighted to have someone to share the responsibility that he didn't want me out of sight. He piled tons of work on me and had to know where I was every minute —this included Saturdays and Sundays—until I put a stop to it."

HEALTH

• Constantly being tired the first few months was a common complaint. Most new managers said they felt they had to spend extra time on the job until they got their feet solidly under them. "There simply aren't enough hours in the day. I take a lot of work home right now and the strain is showing." "I know it will go away, but I now have a lot of sleepless nights trying to solve problems that are larger than I've ever encountered before." "This job is really a change, and I don't have the mechanics down yet. I find it a real strain to take 30 to 40 phone calls a day, see all the people who want to see me, do quick fixes and work on long-range solutions to problems, plus do routine paperwork. Once I learn to manage my time better and become more efficient, the pressure should ease." • The more unfamiliar the

25

job was, the more severe the health problems became. "For the first month, I remember running to the bathroom several times a day to throw up." "I got all caught up in the whirlwind of crisis after crisis, demand after demand, and went home every night unable to relax because I was chainsmoking and drinking four to five pots of coffee a day." "I had a lot of chest pains at first. I really let the pressure sweep me away until I decided either to get myself under control or get the hell out!"

YOUR NEW STATUS AND HOW PEOPLE TREAT YOU BECAUSE OF IT

• "People started making appointments instead of just dropping in." • "It was easier for me to set up meetings. People found fewer reasons not to be there and were more willing to change priorities so they could be in attendance." • "People placed more demands on my time. There was more insistence on seeing *me* instead of the second in command." • "The media was much more interested in what I had to say." • "Sometimes I had a flood of information from people who wanted to overpower me and get something across. At other times, people would censor information or clam up. I couldn't get enough detail to enable me to ask good questions; it made decision making tough." "Colleagues who knew I had more authority started giving me information they never would have shared before." • "I found a lot of people sitting on the fence until they knew where I stood on an issue." • "Since I had the power to make a final decision, some people were incredibly manipulative. They used every trick in the book and every contact they had to influence my decision while staying safely in the background. They even tape-recorded our telephone conversations in case I changed my mind or in the event they wanted to do a little sabotage!"

2. Now That I'm Boss, How Do I Run This Place?

So now you've focused on feelings, attitudes, emotions, frustrations, and circumstances that can accompany you into a new management office. There are some things you can do to lessen the negative impact of it all. You can develop positive strategies that will set the stage for the way you and your management operations are accepted. Managers who fare the best during the difficult early days are those who rely on *action* rather than *emotion* to create positive change. It's fine to be warm, receptive, and helpful, but it's a lot more effective to behave in a strong and confident manner.

Even if your arrival on the scene did not stimulate negative responses and complex problems, look over the following list of tips to smooth the way into your new office. We think you will find them helpful. Choose those you'd like to try.

FIRST DAY ON THE JOB

- Do a quick review of the budget. Collect any existing organizational planning documents.
- Meet the staff around you.
- Get your office set up for *work*. Decorate after hours.
- Start listing the things you think you want to accomplish for the organization.
- Ask your secretary to sort out all junk mail from your correspondence and to put the name of a person on each letter who could help deal with the problem or request.
- Get all meetings or deadlines marked on your calendar.
- You're the boss. Have at it.

MEETING AND DEALING WITH STAFF

- Learn names. Request seating charts (discreetly and unobtrusively) from a trusted aide* when you are in meetings with new staff. Memorize names and jobs before you go "on tour."
- Meet as many people as possible on a one-to-one basis, starting with key staff.
- Visit people in their own bailiwick to learn more about them; squelch the myth that higher-ups never leave their offices.
- Invite people to your office so that they can learn more about you. Include potential antagonists to establish turf.
- When establishing relationships, it is 51 percent up to you and 49 percent up to your staff.
- If you can't visit key staff, telephone them so that they'll know you are around. Don't overdo it, or they'll wish you weren't.
- Until you know how staff members operate, ask why they made the decisions they did.
- If you need to establish yourself and your position, do things for people that will make you valuable.
- Ask for specific help and support. If it is not forthcoming, and if your request is reasonable, lower the boom. Do it calmly and cleverly.

* Using your best intuition and first-impression tools, identify one of this variety the very first day. You may have to reassess your evaluation later, but for now, somebody to help with such details is better than nobody.

- Take corrective action if your staff starts going over your head.
- Get involved in hiring key staff members.
- Immediately get on top of important issues. Establish a methodology for keeping track of them.
- Begin establishing informal grapevines. The sooner they're working, the better.
- Go to the staff meetings of the directors or supervisors who report to you. See how they interact with their own staffs.
- Listen. Listen. Listen. (See *listening*, "The Woman's Glossary.")
- If you write an introductory letter to those in your organization, keep it honest and make your statements general enough that employees won't want to challenge you before you've even hung the pictures on your walls. Save the controversial stuff for face-to-face meetings when you are on firmer ground.

INITIAL STAFF MEETINGS

- Don't meet in large groups until you are ready. But don't delay too long!
- Do not put substantive or complex problems on the first agenda if you are not ready to deal with them or cannot offer some solutions. Set the agenda yourself so that you stay in control.
- Be as certain as possible that you can deliver on any commitments you may make during the meeting.
- Postpone (tactfully) those issues raised by others that you are not prepared to handle. Set a definite time to deal with them, however.
- If possible, announce a major decision you've made or an important new policy or procedure.
- Don't be overly sentimental in your first remarks to the full group. Be pleasant, firm, and businesslike. At the same time, a little warmth will ease tension.

CHOOSING A LEADERSHIP STYLE

- Don't build a mystique that everything can run without you.
- Do some homework. Find out what kind of leadership the organization really needs.

MANAGEMENT STRATEGIES FOR WOMEN

- Consciously pick a style you find comfortable. Be realistic about yourself and the organization when you do so.
- Do not announce your style to others. They may use it against you. Let them learn by seeing—it's more effective that way.
- Avoid pretending you are God. Others know you are not.

STRENGHTENING YOUR POSITION IN THE EARLY WEEKS

- Relax. You're going to mess up somewhere. Just keep the mistake small.
- Refuse to be put on the spot.
- Ask your staff to present major problems and possible solutions to you *in writing*. This gives you a point of departure and lets you know what others are thinking.
- Do not begin your job by sending out memos containing operational rules unless you must. You will look like a controller instead of a leader. These guidelines should come from the personnel or administrative officer.
- If operational plans exist for your area of responsibility, become knowledgeable about them, pick up the reins, and move ahead. If they do *not* exist, begin planning activities so that you know where you are headed, why, and at what cost. (Look back at that list you made the first day which noted things you thought you wanted to accomplish. How do they fit in?)
- Get your performance planning and appraisal processes underway as soon as possible. Help your staff to understand where *they* are headed, why, and at what cost.
- Don't be above asking for advice when you need it.
- Establish directions and priorities *yourself*. Do the initial detailed work *yourself*. You can't turn the ship around with someone else doing the steering.
- Make a list of people you'll need to get to know outside the organization. Start taking some to lunch (see "Food for Business").
- If you delegate responsibility on an interim basis, delegate authority on the same basis.
- Analyze immediately why something failed.
- Don't tell people everything you know or think right off the bat.

- Research other people whom you think are successful. Be with them. Talk with them. Borrow their good ideas. Try to figure out why they are successful in the eyes of others.
- If you hear about someone who has done something well, find out how she made it happen.

BUILDING CONFIDENCE AND TRUST

- Don't tell people they are doing a good job when you think they may not be.
- Find out who has a good analytical mind. As a starter, jot some people a note saying, "What do you recommend we do about. . . ."
- Find out who will disagree with you. "Yes persons" are no good if you truly want help.
- If you're really concerned about whom you can trust, plant a few seeds. Tell someone a confidence that, if revealed, would not hurt the organization. If you hear it again, you'll know who can't keep confidences.
- Lay it on the line. If something needs to be kept quiet for a while, let everyone know. Be straight about the consequences of breaking trust. Follow through if someone finks.

DEALING WITH INSECURITIES

- Don't jump headlong into tough situations without proper briefing and background. In the early weeks, move cautiously and carefully. It will build confidence for later on.
- If some individual really makes you anxious, get to know that person better.
- Get a perspective of others in a job similar to yours.
- Don't spill your insecurities to everyone. Let them think you have it together. As Grandma says, "Thinking is being."
- Remember that people have greater respect for leaders who make mistakes with some degree of decisiveness than leaders who never make mistakes because they never lead.

STRATEGIES WITH THE BOSS

- Don't lie to the boss. She doesn't need you around if you do.
- If she asks you to do something, do it well and ahead of deadline if reasonably possible. If appropriate, add some of your own recommendations.
- After a time, take the initiative by recommending solutions to important problems, including those out of your own area. It will show that you are assertive and not afraid to take risks.
- When it is appropriate, be open about needs, problems, and information.
- Try to understand the boss's position and where you disagree with her. Keep your mouth shut until you know what you're talking about.
- If you're having trouble with the boss making most of the decisions in your area of responsibility, address the problem head-on. Also, begin handling the problems without asking if you can.
- Make a conscious decision not to consult the boss any more than you have to. That way, when you see her, she will know you have something important to discuss.
- If you are unclear about your authority, put *your* understanding in writing and see if the boss agrees.
- Ask your boss about historical and prevailing traps in the organization that could cause you difficulties in getting your job done.

ADDRESSING THE UNFAMILIAR

- Put your nose to the grindstone and immediately learn about the organizational structure, goals, missions, objectives, and key people. (If you're in the public sector, learn the laws governing your activity.)
- Learn who the players are. Watch who talks, who doesn't, who tries to impress others, who tries to snow others.
- Generally, be straightforward if you don't know something. It's imprudent to pretend. Besides, pretenders get caught at the most embarrassing times. Do say you will find the answer and report back. And do so quickly.

- If you suspect that an antagonist is badgering you into admitting ignorance or forcing you into making a decision before you're ready, turn the tables on him. Ask what he knows that you don't, or ask him what he feels is the correct decision. Take it under advisement.
- Ask people inside and outside the organization if there is anything you should know about a particular issue. You'll not only learn something about the issue; you'll learn about *them*.

3. How to Know When You're in a Loser Job and When You're Not

SHE IS comfortable in formal meetings with the President of the United States and cabinet officers; she attends and hosts important events with the nation's most presitigious, most famous, most accomplished people. She is talented, bright, politically astute. And for a long while, she was in a loser job. It paid extremely well, it seemed to have potential, but on the inside of the organization—where it didn't show—forces were at work which made the job a classic no-win situation. Why did she stay?

"I can't *believe* I cannot *make* this thing work! It's too important to me! There has to be an answer."

Success had been her style. Failure had not. "I'm not going to fail. I *can't* fail," she said over and over.

"You are not failing," we told her. "You can neither succeed nor fail when you have no ability to influence the outcome."

There comes a time, and all of us must understand this, when our best effort and greatest commitment have *no power* to influence or change a lost cause. Continuing to struggle drains our personal and professional resources. It can destroy self-confidence.

Do *you* ever get the feeling that you would like to walk out of your office door and never show up on the job again? And, when these feelings strike, do you think:

- Something must be wrong with *me,* because I can't seem to understand what is wanted in this job.
- I'm not qualified to do this job or I'd know how to get (take your choice . . . the committee, the boss, the employees) to take action on my work.
- If I leave, people will think I'm a quitter.
- If I stay put a little longer, everything might work itself out.
- Whatever excuse keeps you from saying to yourself, "It's the job, silly, not me, and it's not worth five years of my life trying to straighten out the situation."

RECOGNIZING LOSER JOBS

There are such things as loser jobs in which capable and talented people just happen to get stuck! However, such jobs are not always immediately or easily discernible.

What follows is a self-test involving typical clues to loser jobs. Examine them carefully, and answer each one true or false as it applies to *your* job. Then refer to Scoring and Total.

_____ 1. Planning is not encouraged or supported. Neither is evaluation of activities.

_____ 2. There are no clearly defined goals for the organization, or for your specific area, and you do not have the authority to set goals and/or direct work toward their achievement.

_____ 3. Above you are power wielders who protect their own, conceal areas of incompetence, and crush innovation and creativity which they find threatening.

_____ 4. There is no effective organizational leadership. People keep asking, "Why are we here? What are we supposed to be about?"

_____ 5. Turnover among officers and senior staff is high; morale everywhere is low.

_____ 6. Policies and procedures are mainly ad hoc and are written not as an operational framework but piece by piece, to solve some immediate need.

_____ 7. Your own position has had a high turnover rate.

_____ 8. Your responsibilities and authority are not clearly defined. It's apparent that no one wants them defined.

_____ 9. You have the feeling that the incompetence around you and/or the politics and pressures are having an adverse effect on your confidence or your health.

_____ 10. You note that other organizations or companies in your field have little respect for yours.

_____ 11. Promises made to you regarding the operation of your department are rarely kept.

_____ 12. No matter how hard you work, it seems as if you never accomplish anything significant.

_____ 13. For whatever reason, you are extremely unhappy or bored in your job, and most days you dread going to work.

_____ 14. No one takes any action on requested reports or tasks that took you days or months to complete. You are confident that the products are of high quality.

_____ 15. The budget for your program has been reduced, perhaps fairly consistently over a period of time.

_____ 16. Most tasks you do are repetitive and call for little creativity or initiative.

_____ 17. You have little chance for advancement or are at the top of your pay grade or professional earning capacity.

_____ 18. You are in an organization that will not support women in high-management jobs.

_____ 19. You are convinced that the purpose behind the established program you are heading is no longer important or needed.

_____ 20. Your boss or board thinks you *must* spend 10 to 12 hours a day at least six days a week to do your job well. You are paid for 40 hours a week.

Scoring

3 points for "true" answers to numbers 3, 9, 12, 13, 19.
2 points for "true" answers to numbers 1, 2, 4, 8, 11, 14, 15, 16, 17, 18, 20.
1 point for "true" answers to numbers 5, 6, 7, 10.

Total

12 points—Time for careful evaluation of your career goals and how your present job is or is not helping you meet them.
13 to 18 points—Start looking.
19 or more points—Start leaving.

RECOGNIZING JOBS THAT AREN'T LOSERS

It is equally important to be able to recognize when you are *not* in a loser job as when you are. If this seems obvious, think about the people you know who have left good jobs for greener pastures only to find that their new fields were not nearly as lush. And remember those who have moaned about going from the employment frying pan into the fire.

There is no doubting it. There are times when it is difficult to recognize positive aspects of a job when the negatives are so apparent and so annoying. Temporary hassles or frustrations may cloud critical success factors. It is necessary, sometimes, to brush aside the surface problems to find the makings of a good future right where you are. If your self-test in the preceding section didn't answer your questions for you, perhaps checking your present job against the following success factors will help. Again, answer each statement true or false; then refer to Total.

_____ 1. There seems to be an effort underway to develop a reasonable master strategy for the future. (This effort may not be apparent at first, given the organization's present struggle to find its own niche in the scheme of things or obvious conflicts between and among certain of the leaders.)

_____ 2. The organization *does* have a sound basis for its compensation program. Salaries appear to be based on performance and objectivity. This means that even if your present salary isn't what you would like, you should have a good opportunity to improve your financial position in the future.

_____ 3. Somewhere up the line there is an open-door policy that allows you to explore your problems and frustrations with the knowledge that someone will at least listen.

_____ 4. Your good works seem to be noticed and appreciated more often than not, even if the right person seems not to notice. ("Right" people often change.)

_____ 5. Employees are encouraged to seek additional training or skill development; in fact, there may be a management development course in-house.

_____ 6. To your knowledge, the company has not experienced a significant number of complaints, personnel grievances, or EEO (Equal Employment Opportunity) actions from employees, whether filed formally or not.

_____ 7. Although your job duties have not been clearly spelled out, there appears to be some general understanding of what is wanted from you. Chances are that if you initiate a statement of responsibilities and authorities from *your* perspective, it will receive a fair hearing.

_____ 8. To your knowledge, the company is on sound financial footing. There seems to be nothing looming on the horizon that would cause a drastic change in the company's potential for reasonable financial growth in the years ahead.

_____ 9. You like the general area of your work, whether it's communications, research, manufacturing, whatever.

_____ 10. You feel as if you are accomplishing something significant on the job.

_____ 11. The work you are doing, in spite of annoyances brought about by bureaucractic or organizational nonsense, is more often than not satisfying to you.

_____ 12. Looking around you, you find that the problems you are encountering seem to be shared as much by men as they are by other women.

_____ 13. A number of employees who have been with the organization for some time appear to be loyal and to have a commitment to the organization, even if they, too, grumble about policies and procedures.

_____ 14. The job does not seem to drain you to an unreasonable degree. Most often, you are ready for a pleasant evening with family and friends at the end of the working day.

_____ 15. You have no serious difficulty in making ends meet on your present income; in fact, you're moving ahead of the game.

_____ 16. Your job is located in a geographical area that matches your feelings about commuting; your ability to pay for transportation is no problem.

Total

There are 16 factors. If 9 or more apply to you, you had better think carefully before moving around—unless, of course, the ideal job offer has just come your way. If 6 to 8 factors apply, chances for your job to develop into something more satisfying are fair. Below that, it's anyone's guess!

4. The Management Leper
How to Tell When You're Not Wanted in an Organization

"TURKEY FARMING," perfected by the Federal government and practiced in both the public and private sectors, was not developed by the Department of Agriculture. It came instead from another major department of the Washington, D.C., bureaucracy. The concept is really fairly simple: When you want to get rid of a highly paid manager and you do not want to undergo the legal and union problems that would result from firing the individual, you put him on the "farm." Normally, this means assignment to a specific project for which there may be no budget other than salary, no staff other than, perhaps, clerical assistants, and, sometimes, no interest in whether or not any work is ever done.

Not every attempt to put an executive or manager out to

pasture is so blatant and discussed as widely in the media as is the Federal government's turkey enterprise. Some attempts are more subtle, and some, believe it or not, are more obvious. And sometimes, when you are in the middle, it is difficult to see either the forest or the trees, let alone the turkeys nesting nearby.

The previous chapter focused on the *job* and its status in the organization; this focuses on *you* and your status there. It's important to recognize the distinction.

Just for fun—and perhaps for enlightenment—look over the following real-life situations. We have promised not to reveal from whom we gleaned these first-person experiences. But believe us, they really have happened! Have they happened to you? There is no Leper Rating. Use your judgment.

1. Your desk (or your office) has been moved several times over the past year, and each location is worse than the last.
2. When you try to discuss your problems with higher-ups, they put you off by saying a reorganization is pending. Then they wink.
3. You ask a subordinate if he has anything important you should know. He hands you a list of social security numbers for new employees (or something equally irrelevant).
4. You discover other employees have been collecting what they consider to be damaging information about you.
5. Staff take turns sitting in your office chair when you are not in your office and sometimes when you are.
6. Someone comes in to measure your office while you are there.
7. You are chosen the person to represent the company at all out-of-town meetings or celebrations addressed to "or a designee."
8. Frequently, you are not allowed to represent the company at a meeting relating to your area of expertise.
9. The door to your office has been removed.
10. You are put in charge of greeting all non-VIPs. These are your only trips to the airport. Your own requests for travel are denied.
11. You call a meeting and nobody comes; you have a party with free drinks and everybody comes.

41

12. Your hairdresser is the first to tell you she's sorry to hear you are not employed anymore. You didn't know you weren't.
13. You speak at a meeting and everyone interrupts you.
14. You make motions at a meeting and nobody will second them.
15. You find your nickname is the Bionic Turkey (or some equally unflattering term).
16. All of your regular duties are removed and you are assigned to a special task force that does nothing. Or you are excluded from assignment to task forces and committees you *should* be on.
17. The lock has been changed on your office door and you aren't given a key.
18. Your telephone has been "temporarily" disconnected for five months and you must use your secretary's line.
19. You find your dictation has been erased from the tape but your correspondence has not been brought in for signature. It seems to have been "lost."
20. You notice that everyone is casually whispering the location of the restaurant or club to which they are going after the meeting. You sheepishly ask where the party is and, naturally, are told everyone is going straight home. Ha!
21. It is almost impossible to get an appointment to see the boss. Your calls to him are not always returned, and when they are, they are days late.
22. Some staff have been taken away from you; the rest are making inquiries about a transfer.
23. Other managers are allowed to make decisions for your area. Sometimes you aren't even told of those decisions until you encounter their ramifications.

5. Power, Power, Who's Got the Power?

ARE *power* and *authority* synoymous? Absolutely not. There is a difference between the two, and recognizing and understanding that difference is critical to the success or failure of any manager. Managers must understand the nature and characteristics of these two organizational phenomena if they intend to accomplish anything worthwhile. Further, an effective manager should have some ideas for getting close to authority and power sources as well as the ability to recognize ways of avoiding dangerous and unsuccessful paths to these two forces.

AUTHORITY VERSUS POWER

Authority may be defined as the right to give commands or take action. This definition implies that there is a relationship between two or more individuals—one, the boss, the others, subordinates. Herbert Simon expresses this relationship clearly and directly: "The superior forms and transmits decisions with the expectation that they will be accepted by the subordinate. The subordinate expects such decisions, and his conduct is determined by them."* Job descriptions reflect this kind of relationship, indicating which buck is to stop at what place. Organizational charts are drawn up in painstaking detail to differentiate between the Big Cheese, little bosses, and tiny underlings and to show who can give an order to whom. And everyone, meanwhile, is trying to get her name into a little box higher up on the chart so that she can say, "Look what I have the right to do."

Authority has limitations. The right to give orders or commands will not ensure that they always will be carried out. An employee whose box is lower down on the organizational chart can squelch an order from higher up if he has the right mixture of followers and persuasive influence. Or if the boss does not use her authority effectively—giving too many orders, or conflicting and confusing orders—the result will be confusion, not compliance. A boss also may exercise the do-it-because-I'm-the-boss-and-I-said-so type of authority ploy only to find half-hearted and sloppy compliance.

Another very realistic and troublesome limitation to authority is one that flies directly in the face of Simon's expectations regarding the functions of superior and subordinates. Well-intentioned management guidelines, either negotiated or legally prescribed, often can be abused. A subordinate who will not accept reasonable assignments, who will not agree to counseling

---

* Herbert A. Simon, *Administrative Behavior: A Study of Decision-Making Processes in Administrative Organization*, 2d ed. (New York: Free Press, 1957).

or training to improve unsatisfactory performance, and who insists upon making trouble constantly may nonetheless be almost impossible to fire.

The greatest limitation of authority, however, is that a manager does not have the right to exercise orders over *everyone* (thank God!).

This leads us into the discussion on power. For many decisions or opportunities, a manager needs the assistance of others outside her realm of subordinates as well as the cooperation of those inside. A prime example is one with which Americans are quite familiar. The President of the United States has the authority to propose a new law, but he may not have the power to get it enacted. A U.S. senator, with the same authority, may be able to use his influence with Congress to get his proposed legislation passed without difficulty.

Chester Barnard defines power as "the capacity to secure the dominance of one's values or goals."* It is a definition worth pondering. Power is influence. For the manager, it is essential to build influence through positive, carefully planned means in order to gain power. And power is essential to authority. It's as simple—and as difficult—as that.

To summarize: One must have both authority (the *right* to take action) and power (the *ability* to influence). Further, to be an effective manager, one must be able to identify and get close to those individuals inside and outside the organization who have authority and power. One must do this to accomplish her business goals and to make her working relationships strong and productive.

QUICK GUIDES TO GETTING CLOSE TO POWER AND AUTHORITY SOURCES

First, you should map out *your* situation by allowing for four factors: (1) What do you want to do? (2) Who has the authority

* Chester Barnard, *The Functions of the Executive* (Cambridge: Harvard University Press, 1956).

to make the final decision? (3) Who has the power to influence that decision? (4) What is your strategy for influencing the authority and power sources?

What you'll want to do is make up a working paper that will look something like this:

WHAT	AUTHORITY	POWER	STRATEGY
_____	_____	_____	_____
		_____	_____
		_____	_____

The Power column has more lines than Authority, because most often the Authority person is a single, easily identified individual. The more complex or important the decision, the more people the Authority person probably will consult or involve. List their names in the Power column as you identify them. Next, design your strategies for success. Use the techniques described in our discussion of *persuasive communication* or, if appropriate, *negotiation* (see "The Woman's Glossary"). You will need to deal with individuals who feel they have some reason to be affected by the decision or who are acting as advisors to the final decision-making authority. For each strategy you design, ask yourself two questions: (1) How would I react if I were the other person? (2) If I am the other person, how does this benefit me; what's in it for me?

Some techniques you can use to identify Power people are these:

- Who is calling you up just to "sniff around" the general topic?
- Who are the "whiz kids" off whom the Authority bounces her best ideas?
- Who are the experts in the field?
- Who is it that the Authority sees socially from the office?
- Who frequently drops into the Authority's office unannounced?

- Who will be affected by the decision?
- Who are the individuals to whom the Authority assigns major problems?

If you are a top executive, you may need to go outside the organization to pinpoint Authority and Power people. Once you think you know who has the right to make a decision, you probably will want to scout around to find out if she or he *really* is the person on whom to spend your energy. Try having your secretary or a subordinate call the outside organization with a tough question in your area of concern and see to whom your caller is referred. It may tell you who *really* does the work or decision making in that area.

SAFE PATHS TO AUTHORITY AND POWER

AUTHORITY

As in anything else, there are many avenues you can take in your quest for power and authority. Some are safer than others. We think the following tips will be helpful.

- If you are given a responsibility, insist that the authority to carry it out comes with it.
- If it is unclear who has the authority to do a certain task or make a decision, assume it is yours if it seems within your area of management and unless someone tells you differently. If you do a good job, chances are the authority will become yours permanently. Turf building? Of course.
- If something is within your authority to do, then *exercise that right* or someone else will assume your prerogative.
- Be very careful about giving committees, boards, commissions, or councils any of your authority. Avoid establishing decision-making groups; keep them advisory. If you do not, you may find yourself responsible for activities over which you have no control.

- If you want more authority in a particular area and if that authority is vested in a council, board, or committee, get yourself appointed to it. Do not be content with an auxiliary position. Be assertive; as the authority switches from one group to another, go with it.
- If you have a desire to obtain more authority, either absorb it if unclaimed, go to the next rung on the organizational ladder, or do a lateral transfer inside or outside the business. The first is more rapid and devoid of the "horribles" of getting a new job. (Read Michael Korda's book *Power, How to Get It, How to Use It*, particularly, the chapter "Expand, Don't Climb.")

POWER

- Be valuable. Try to discover what things you can do for someone that they cannot do or are afraid to do. After you have identified what people need, then provide it. (Examples of needs could be information, contacts, sources of money, services, good public relations, negotiation, persuasion.)
- Be selective about how you use your own influence. Overuse erodes its effectiveness. Make each time count.
- Cultivate your ability to deal with complex situations. It doesn't matter what amount of authority you have; if you cannot cope, you cannot have influence.
- Learn to be controlled in adverse situations. It will help others perceive you as calm and capable under stress.
- Laughter is power. It does not mean that a person denies the existence of misery if she laughs; she simply pretends to be victorious over it. Laughter also demonstrates the ability to transcend the tragic horizon of self-involvement and personal affront.
- Be around Power people. It gives you a chance to observe their modus operandi. Borrow their good methods; avoid their bad ones.
- Give credit where credit is due. The extension of this courtesy helps avoid anger and resistance to you and may even protect you against rebellion in the future. It also keeps the troops happy.
- Avoid the display of power symbols that make you look like a

carbon copy of everyone else or a rider of coattails. Go for individuality.

- Everything you think should not come out of your mouth. Power people cannot be easily read.
- Practice active listening (see *listening*, "The Woman's Glossary"). Quietly check out anything disturbing. But while you have an ear to the track, keep your head up so you can see as well as hear; some of the most powerful people are quiet in their moves.
- If you are a member of a power group and are the only woman around, try getting another woman into the fold. That way you can give power to each other if the men are not willing to give it to you. (See "Tokenism in Management.")
- Assess your power once a year. There is a fine line between people who come to you because they like you and those who come to you because you can do something for them. You want both kinds of support. Do you have a good balance here?
- Increased power comes from being responsible for or doing something significant. It is foolish to want more power without giving thought to whether it is deserved and what you will do with it when you have it.
- If someone owes you some chips, be selective as to when you cash in. It is more advantageous to have someone indebted to you than you to him.

DANGEROUS PATHS TO POWER AND AUTHORITY

- Trying to get power or authority at real cost to others. (See Don't spit into the wind, "Maxims to Operate and Succeed By.")
- Thinking you have to be like a man to be his equal. Why not try your own approach and style? If he is a student of male writings on management, he will be thrown off-guard—to your advantage.
- Reading books on power that insinuate women will never have it. Go ahead and read them for others' game plans, but when finished, toss them before paranoia sets in. Now go out and get the power in your own way.
- Carelessly delegating authority which you must keep to be effective. Middle managers especially should exercise caution on this point. Once given up, authority is difficult to retrieve.
- Trying to establish personal relationships by gossiping about

others. Bring only news of appropriate nature to the organization.

- Giving personal confessions or secret confidences to Authority and Power people in an effort to gain rapport or favor. For middle managers, such actions turn bosses into unwanted parent, sibling, protector figures. It's an invitation.
- Jumping into the rat race before you have first watched others and evaluated their behavior. Breaking the informal rules and mores of an organization can be just as embarrassing and deadly as breaking official policies or regulations. Mess-ups make you stick out like an inexperienced clod.
- Going over your boss's head without telling him/her—another caution especially germane for middle managers. Such characters often go far—out the door.

6. The Woman's Glossary
Selected Terms Designed to Make You a Better Communicator

EFFECTIVE COMMUNICATION is an art. It is also a skill which must be mastered if one is to become a successful manager. Standing in the way of clear, direct communication are buzzwords and deceptive behaviors. Some are placed in our way unintentionally; others, deliberately.

To address this problem, we have developed a glossary of terms to assist managers in two ways. One way is by providing helpful information on communication behaviors, methods, processes, and systems. The other is by defining confusing buzzwords which may be confronted on the job. Reading the information on the following pages will sharpen your communications skills and will help you recognize when someone is trying to confuse or impress you through the use of buzzwords.

aggressive communication   Using behaviors and words that are accusatory, belittling, superior, and which usually have a negative effect on others. Discouraging honest responses from others through intimidation and bullying communications tactics. Differs from *assertive communication* in substance, style, and results.

assertive communication   Stating one's wants, wishes, feelings directly and with honesty. Encouraging responses of the same nature through attentive listening and positive, caring behavior. Differs from *aggressive communication* in substance, style, and results.

body language   Expressions, messages, signs, signals sent by the human body other than through use of words. Avoidance or ignorance of these communications signals lessens one's ability to pick up on what's being silently stated.

buzzword   Normally, a word of esoteric nature, often used to confuse or confound; a specialized or technical word which may be a hybrid of other more commonly understood words. Buzzwords may be encountered in almost every profession, and should be treated with caution, if not suspicion.

communications breakdown   A break or hiatus in the process of communication. At the top of the list of excuses for anything that goes wrong in the organization. Can be minimized by providing good communications training programs for the organization, by establishing appropriate formal communications structures, and by refusing to accept the phenomenon as an excuse.

communications gap   Inability to understand the content of a message. Widely used to explain why certain managers avoid meaningful communication with each other. A communications gap may happen by design, through the use of falsehood, ambiguity, misleading information. Or it may happen by accident.

distortion   A change, usually undesired, in a message. Example: On learning that there would be an *average* merit raise of 7 percent this year, Manager X explained to her staff that there would be a *maximum* raise of 7 percent, an inadvertent (and morale-shattering) distortion.

feedback   In bureaucratese, the return of a portion of the output of any process or system to the input, especially when used to maintain the output within predetermined limits. (Good grief!) More generally, a response to something. It seems that in modern American government, business, or academia, it is impossible to function without frequent use of this term, or nearly so. The term is only slightly more useful than *input* and *output*, which are often used with it. We encourage the use of the process, but recommend describing it by any means other than that used in the first sentence.

gobbledygook   Verbose, bureaucratic, muddied, and muddled communication. The word comes from *gobble,* the sound that turkeys make, which tells us something about gobbledygook. *Gook* means a sludgy substance, which tells us even more. The *Washington Star* newspaper runs a regular column of gobbledygook, a practice which has called attention to nonsense in business communication. Public display of turkey talk seems to reduce its incidence.

input   A contribution from one source or individual to another; often an idea, recommendation, opinion, plan. (See *output, feedback.*) The excessive use of this word often irritates others.

interface   Surprise! This is *not* an activity. It is a surface which forms a common bond or boundary between adjoining regions. Remember the definition next time someone invites you to interface.

interference   The act of interfering. A communications buzzword for inaccurate or distorted information either intentionally or unintentionally placed in the way of the receiver. (See *distortion, rumor.*) Football players receive penalties for interference; the same concept might well be considered by businesses.

jawbone   To discuss, debate, explore verbally; to brainstorm. Extensively used by politicians and other promoters in place of more accurate, widely understood terms. May be confused with, or related to, a part of an ass.

listening   Applying oneself to hearing something. The communications complement is *speaking.*

Listening is learning. *Supportive listening* is a key to leadership and success. This means (1) listening patiently, (2) expressing understanding of other person's feelings and perspectives, and (3) using questions to reinforce understanding, to ascertain that you have heard correctly, and to get additional information. Some examples follow:

1. *Listening patiently.* George has difficulty finishing a sentence. It's tempting to help out by supplying words or thoughts. This constitutes jumping to a conclusion George may not have intended; also, it encourages his habit of not completing what he has started to say. Further, George often talks around the subject. It takes time and patience to get to the substance of the issue. Impatience may destroy any possibility of identifying what is wrong and finding a solution.

2. *Expressing understanding of the other person's feelings.* "I'm furious with Shirley," a peer tells you. "She drives every Thursday, and every Thursday our whole carpool is late." Your response: "I know how angry you must feel. Being late gets the day off to a bad start."

3. *Using questions.* "There isn't enough time allocated to this portion of the work plan. We'll never be able to meet the deadline," a supervisor complains to you. Your question (which really isn't a question at all): "You believe there isn't enough time to do the work?"

The question indicates that you have been listening and, in a nonthreatening way, encourages additional information from the supervisor.

memorandum A form of written communication most often used within an organization, or sometimes used between organizations to outline the terms of an agreement—a "memorandum of understanding."

Memos are sometimes described as being brief messages, which, in fact, they should be. Keeping a memo as brief as possible is only one of the ground rules for succeeding in the memoranda melee.

Before sending a memo, make certain that the business at hand truly necessitates putting information in writing at this time. Determine to whom the information *must* be sent, limit copies only to those who *should* know, and keep information to the point.

It is a fact of business behavior that most people who receive memos often question their origin. "Why send a memo?" "Why didn't she discuss this with me in person?" "Why did she copy my boss?" Probably the most frequently raised speculation about a memo is that it was written to cover the sender's derrière.

Some individuals use memoranda to mislead, maneuver, and malign. Watch out for these memo monsters. Here is an example: Manager A meets with Manager B, at B's request, to discuss an idea of B's. Manager A compliments B on her idea, raises no questions, and gives verbal support for her and for her plan. Hours later, B receives a memo which strongly criticizes the idea, insults B's intelligence in a subtle way, and warns that support from A will not be forthcoming. B's boss (a vice president), the president, and other officers are sent copies of A's surprising attack.

B's immediate reaction is to write a lengthy defense of her idea and of herself. A secondary reaction probably will be to recognize that the idea and its merit are not the issue and to feel that a one-liner might be the best response: "Your memo takes a point of view entirely opposite that which you expressed during our meeting."

B should avoid the temptation to write *any* response. If she responds, A will then fire back a memo saying he cannot understand how she so *totally* misinterpreted his initial remarks. By this time, the president and officers are annoyed and could not care less how all of this started. When the time is appropriate, B can present her idea and its justification to the right people in a positive, productive way.

If B had written a memo immediately following her meeting with A, outlining her understanding of that meeting, would it have helped? Probably not. It is likely that A would have responded with sarcasm, noting the difference between his "recollection" and hers. In some instances, a follow-up memo of this nature is helpful; with a strategist like A, it seldom is. As Grandpa would say, "Don't get into a hissing contest with a snake," or something like that.

negotiation   The art of legitimate compromise. The process of reaching agreement; a clearly understood and mutually agreed-upon process of conferring or discussing.

Never enter into a negotiation process unless you have full understanding of the nature and priority of your own terms: (1) those that *must not* be sacrificed, (2) those that can be given up, (3) those that can be traded in the negotiating process. In addition, do enough homework so that you have a reasonable idea of how the opposition has categorized his terms. Have a feel for what his priorities are.

Within the second and third categories (above), always determine priorities. Since terms in the first category cannot be given up, there is no need to establish negotiation priorities. A skillful negotiator will play her hand like a riverboat gambler, recognizing the value of each card in her hand and knowing what it will bring her. She also has a good idea of how the man across the table will play his cards.

The only time a successful negotiator shows emotion other than calmness is by design. Indignation or impatience, at the right time, may do wonders.

When is a program manager most likely to need negotiations skills? Each time she has to defend and/or modify her budget.

networks   Communications chains linking individuals or places, either of a formal or informal nature. Processes, systems, or structures established within an organization to organize collection and dissemination of information or to describe *reporting responsibilities or assignments.* Informally established, a strategy for sharing information among members of a group with common interests.

Your organization has a formal communications network in place. Should you establish an informal structure? Yes. Always. Most managers admit that the company grapevine carries more information than the formal system. Your own network can be enormously helpful in providing support (particularly to the women in an organization); running down rumors; testing ideas; influencing others regarding plans, individuals, systems. An informal network has its own ground rules— candor, honesty, loyalty. A way of building these characteristics is to share openly and honestly with the members of your network, to display concern for their ideas and welfare, and to *earn* their trust rather than expect it.

noise   A disturbance that obscures or reduces the clarity and quality of a message. *Rumors* are sometimes considered noise in the communications process.

nonverbal communication   Communication by means other than spoken words, such as facial expressions, gestures, signals, signs, attitudes, behaviors. (See *body language.*) People communicate in a variety of ways, and managers especially should keep this in mind. When someone is consistently late to meetings, breaks luncheon dates, forgets to file reports, that someone is communicating an obvious message. So also is the staff member who is often ill and away from the office when tough decisions must be made. The executive who keeps her office door open and expects you to enter without knocking, even when she is on the telephone, is telling you much about herself. Whether or not you feel comfortable entering an office under such circumstances tells her much about you.

obfuscate   To render indistinct or dim; to confuse. A high-level manager we know throws *obfuscate* at every new kid on the management block. He accuses them of obfuscating the issue, any issue, then sits back and waits. Pity the new arrival who does not know what it is that she supposedly has done to the issue. A good answer, of course, is to respond that the accuser is, himself, behaving in an obfuscatory manner. Or one could accuse him of *tergiversating.*

observing   Perceiving, noticing, seeing, watching attentively. It is extremely important to be able to receive messages sent by means other than words—body language, behaviors, various signals. Learning to be a keen observer is well worth the time and a rather fascinating effort. It requires moving out of self and tuning in to others. Pick up on the technique and you'll pick up on a lot that you may have been missing. Practice observing others, even passers-by.

one-way communication A message sent from one person, thing, or place to another without response. Positive characteristics of one-way communication are that it is fast, orderly, and may occur in an environment less confusing than does two-way communication. The most significant negative characteristic is that it is less accurate than two-way communication because it does not provide for discussion and clarification in the communications process.

organizational distance The combined result of normal losses in transmission and protective screening. In garden-variety English, this is usually described as a situation where "something is lost in the translation." Protective screening indicates the act of removing or altering information from the message which might be harmful in the judgement of the person doing the removing or altering. A staff member may leave out details which would indicate lax performance on his part when he briefs you on his activities. Combine these willful miscommunications with normal loss in transmission and there can be a real problem. There are, however, better and more easily understood ways of describing these circumstances than by using the term *organizational distance.* At least in our book.

output The product of one or more inputs. (See *input, feedback.*) No, output is not the last of the puts. From Washington, D.C., came a middleput of sorts called "thruput." While we are quite willing to deal with in and out, we are not yet ready to deal with thru. Thus, our put family has a missing linkput.

person-to-person communication, or one-on-one communication An exchange of information, discussion, or sharing that takes place between two individuals. (See *two-way communication, persuasive communication, negotiation.*)

Even managers who can speak effectively to groups or on a podium may have difficulty in a one-on-one exchange. It may be that the exchange aspect is missing, with the manager delivering her message and neither providing for nor encouraging remarks from the other person. Other problems involve half-listening, emotional feelings about the issue at hand or about the other person, failure to recognize how the other individual views you and/or your power, jumping to conclusions, differing perspectives, and failure to make clear, direct statements. (Speaking to the point and supportive listening are discussed under *speaking* and *listening.*)

MANAGEMENT STRATEGIES FOR WOMEN

Some helpful tips are these:

1. Prepare yourself for an important person-to-person exchange; don't try to wing it.
2. Try to understand emotional barriers that might be in the way of clear communication. If someone is upset, help him express his feelings before addressing the issue. Take care only to listen; don't place judgement on the feelings.
3. Recognize that the other person may have a perspective that differs from yours. Role play in your mind. If you were he, what would be your reaction to what he is about to hear?
4. Apply yourself when listening. Send back information to make certain you both know that you understand what you have been told.
5. Always note points of agreement or understanding before raising points of disagreement.
6. If it is a critical issue, allow sufficient time to air it *thoroughly* and to consider alternative solutions or directions. Let the other person know that his contribution is important to you and worth your time.

persuasive communication Communicating with the purpose of reaching an agreement based on logic, reasoning, and thorough examination of an issue. A logical process: not manipulation.

Don't confuse persuasive communication with manipulation or with forcing someone to a conclusion. Agreement comes about through a process which requires that you:

1. Be as specific as possible. Quantify so that others are able to weigh various alternatives in the decision-making process.
2. Do your homework. No one is going to accept your point of view if she suspects that it's based on poor research.
3. Speak directly to the point. Be concise. Present arguments in a logical sequence so that they are more easily understood.
4. Emphasize points of agreement.
5. Clarify points of disagreement. Explore objections in great detail, drawing out others' points of view and attempting to understand. Seek understanding of your perspective.
6. Be honest, open, and aboveboard. Keep no cards under the table, up your sleeve, or in the hole. This is one time it will not pay off.

public speaking The act of making a verbal presentation, usually in a formal sense, before an audience; most often, presenting a message to a special interest group on a topic related specifically to that interest.

There is abundant information available on how to address a group —how to speak, how to dress, whether to use notes, how to move on the platform. For our purpose, which is to provide key how-to tips, we offer what we believe to be the most helpful and important guidelines. For the woman whose legs still need support hose to get them to the platform after all of this, we suggest a short course in public speaking.

First, be yourself. Be as natural as you possibly can. Your comfort will make others comfortable. Second, *plan, practice,* and *perfect* your presentation, unless the occasion is informal and spontaneity and improvisation are indicated. Once you have mastered your presentation, put it aside until time to speak. Don't do and redo until you are undone.

Here are some basic organizational tips:

1. Know the make-up of your audience.
2. Make certain you know how much time you will have for your total presentation. If the topic and audience warrant, allow time for a question-and-answer period at the conclusion of your speech.
3. Use an organizational scheme appropriate to your topic. If you are discussing the cost of America's energy, you may want to organize on a historical basis: past, present, future. You may prefer to organize the topic on a geographical basis: cost of energy produced in Alaska, the West, off-shore, the Arab oil countries. You may want to organize around the *kinds* of energy and their cost: oil, electricity, coal, solar power, wind power, synthetic fuels.

   If you are discussing the status of women, you again might choose a historical framework: past, present, future. Or a more interesting presentation might result from a different organization: the economic, legal, political, social status.

   In addition to historical and geographical frameworks, there are a number of others you can use to help in the organization of the body of your message. They include pro/con, cause/effect, problem/solution.

   Of course your speech will have an *introduction* preceding the kind of information described above and a *conclusion* following it.

4. What should be included in the introduction? Greetings to the audience, an explanation of the purpose of your presence, and a statement identifying yourself with the special interest of the audience. Most speakers use pleasantries and humor interspersed with their more serious introductory remarks. Unless there is some very strong reason not to do so, or unless you feel uncomfortable with humor, use these devices. They are effective.

5. Conclude something; don't just end. Use a reiteration of your principal points to build a logical conclusion, observation, or forecast. Your conclusion should be pithy and to the point; it should not drag on. Make it a zinger. End with a "thank you."

6. Dress like a professional. It will do a lot for the audience, but more for you.

reading Comprehending, or taking in the meaning of, something printed or written. The communications complement is *writing*.

At this age, who needs to be reminded about reading? Who needs a *definition*, for pity sakes? Most of us do! Reread the definition: comprehending, or taking in the meaning of. . . . How often we read with half attention, neither comprehending nor trying to take in the meaning of what we are reading! It is our firm belief that a major key to success is learning to read with agility and comprehension.

A woman who recently was named chairperson of the board of a prestigious, highly visible corporation whose work extends to every state in the Union reads *every* word written about *every* facet of the business. We think she became chairperson because she knew more than any of her fellow board members. And she knew more because she read more—*really* read more!

Another woman we know is a state senator. She also reads every word of everything germane to her work. She can politick far better than the average senator because she really *knows* what's going on. Some executive branch departments intent on snowing the legislature have to clean up their own snow when they try to obfuscate the scene. The reading senator will blow the whistle.

There is far too much paper to read, you say? Of course there is. So learn to read faster and with greater comprehension. There are people who can teach you how, but the habit of reading for comprehension is one you can develop by yourself with practice. It's serious business, this learning to read, and not just for children in school!

receiving   Taking or acquiring something given, offered, or transmitted. The communications complement is *transmitting*. Individuals communicating via radio often inquire of each other, "Are you receiving me?" While this is not the question we would normally ask others with whom we are communicating, it is helpful to test the quality of reception through other, more specific questions related to the message. Don't assume, just because you are sending, that someone else is receiving. Find out.

reporting responsibilities, assignments   Responsibility of an individual to send and receive relevant information to and from specified positions within an organization.

In traditional organizational structures, this means that a supervisor must keep her manager appropriately informed and must be appropriately informed about the activities of her own staff. In the event that information is received that should have gone to her manager, the supervisor is required to see that the information goes to the manager accurately and expeditiously.

The supervisor normally is expected to report according to the chain of command within her organization, not skipping over her boss to go to a higher authority. Under certain circumstances, she may risk such action if the chance appears good for acceptance of her message and her behavior. Sometimes, when an individual has a terrific idea and her manager and others reject it out of hand, she will gamble on it and go to the top. But she should understand the risks. If the idea makes a million dollars for the company and she becomes a vice president, the risk was worth it. If she loses her job for insubordination or whatever, it may not have been.

If our supervisor is having difficulty with a peer, she will discuss that difficulty with her manager, who will discuss it with the peer's manager.

Communication downward is of critical importance. To ensure that her staff is well informed, she probably will establish regular staff meetings with a structured agenda and an open-discussion period for each. She will make certain that her staff members understand their responsibilities to report relevant information to her. Further, she probably will schedule a regular time for each project director or unit to report progress and problems, allowing enough time for full discussion.

If at any time there is doubt about her responsibility to provide or receive reports, she immediately will request a clarification to avoid a *communications breakdown.*

rumor A message generally based on speculation, anticipation, gossip. It results from a distortion in the communications process and is sometimes called *noise*. The best defense against the rumor is a well-designed formal communications network coupled with an efficiently operating informal network.

It is wise to think twice before responding to a rumor. There may be several reasons for the occurrence of an item of misinformation. These can include mischief making, insecurity among employees, or anxiety of one sort or another. On the other hand, rumors sometimes develop because people are rushed, too busy, and simply do not get a message straight. Move carefully before challenging anyone or taking action you may regret.

Always be on guard, however, for those people who "accidently" or "mistakenly" or "humorously" peddle false information. It doesn't take long to identify most people of this type, but some are very clever. (See List of Dangerous Characters, "Who Lurks There?")

Openly discussing current rumors with your trusted informal network is a good way to give them exposure and to learn a great deal about their origin and the extent of their dissemination. This is according to one school of thought. The other school insists that one should never repeat or even refer to a rumor when an attempt is being made to squelch or refute it. Instead, the idea is to issue a positive statement that clears up the issue without reference to the original gossip. However, this is sometimes difficult, especially if the rumor concerns situations about which no one is ready to provide the true scoop, or any scoop, for that matter.

signaling Communicating through the use of signs, gestures, behaviors. The communications complement is *observing*. Recognizing others' signals is a critical communications skill. And those signals may not be as obvious as Boy Scout flags.

speaking Expressing oneself verbally. The communications complement is *listening* (or *observing*, if the "listener" is a lip reader). (See *public speaking, persuasive communication, person-to-person communication*.)

Always speak to the point. We often tend to build a case for the point we want to make, explain it, or defend it before letting our listener know what that point is. By the time we have reached the point, the listener already has jumped to a conclusion—probably the wrong one. How much better it is to say what is important up front, then to add background information. Speaking to the point is key to communicating effectively.

static See *noise*. In addition, a very helpful term for letting others know when you believe they are communicating irrelevancies: "Quit the static. Give me concrete examples."

tergiversate Here is your own buzzword to drop on others whenever the occasion is right. To tergiversate is to change one's attitudes or opinions with respect to cause or subject, to practice evasion, to dodge, to prevaricate. The tergiversator is a highly competent specialist at confusing the issue.

transmitting Sending from one thing, person, or place to another. The communications complement is *receiving*. Abundant information is being transmitted every day from this place to that, with the result that people sometimes feel as if they are drowning in paper. We suggest that, as in writing a memo, you take care to determine before you transmit any information that it is necessary to do so. Remember, diseases also are *transmitted*. Don't spread unnecessary information and infect others with a rash of unwanted paper.

two-way communication A communications process which provides for response, exchange, sharing in reaction to a given message. Characteristics of two-way communication are that it is more accurate, less orderly, and slower than one-way communication. The reason for these differences is the discussion/clarification nature of two-way communication.

verbal communication Communication of, pertaining to, or associated with words. How you use words can influence others almost as much as the meaning of the words. A favorite cousin used words as an artist uses colors—to form exactly the picture she wanted, to make a composition that appealed to the senses as well as to the mind. She chose her words carefully, and treated them well. This does not mean she was too wordy or verbose—far from it. For our part, we started a collection of words that were new and interesting to us, defined them in writing, and added them to our vocabulary. Collecting words is a marvelous hobby and one that can pay off on the way "upstairs."

writing Putting words (or symbols) on paper or other writing surface with the intention that they be *read*.

Business writing is the topic of entire academic courses. If a new manager has doubts about her ability to write clearly, concisely, accurately—even creatively—we recommend a crash course in the subject. And yes, business writing *can* be creative. How you express yourself in your business correspondence and written reports tells others a lot about you, just as you judge others from their writings. Some basic ground rules are these:

1. Recognize the importance of solid writing skills; do whatever necessary to develop them.
2. Purge all written business communications of pettiness, meanness, or insulting remarks; otherwise, these remarks will come back to haunt you.
3. Work for clarity and preciseness to reduce misunderstanding.
4. Whatever you do, make certain that written materials that leave your office or command are grammatically correct and error free. Nothing distracts so much from the quality of an idea as to have it expressed poorly.

7. Who Lurks There?
Dangerous, Bothersome, and Priceless Characters

THERE ARE characters in every organization who have sorry afflictions in their personalities or modus operandi. These folks should be ejected from their jobs just as soon as it is determined that they have little or no salvage value and that keeping them is prolonging the inevitable.

Other office eccentrics are simply bothersome and need a frank session or two to alter their performance. These individuals have the potential for change.

The priceless folks comprise a third set of office characters—executives should do almost anything to keep them.

How well do you know the characters who work for you? Help yourself understand them with our lists of the good, bad, and the ugly in an organization. The purpose of this test is not to develop a nascent paranoia. It is, instead, to assist you in honestly evaluating the human side of your work situation. We hope that this exercise will also encourage you to ask yourself if you are the cause of negative or positive performance of your employees. Since your response to the following lists should remain private, you can record actual names. Do this on first impulse and later analyze *your* influence on their behavior!*

LIST OF DANGEROUS CHARACTERS†

DIRECTIONS: Each paragraph that follows describes characteristics of a dangerous person in an organization. Recall situations where these traits were displayed by a worker. Name the person or persons.

EXPLANATION: Depending on your own values, some of the situations are severe enough to warrant their happening only once before you consider dismissing the individual. The situation is serious when the behavior has become a dangerous and predictable pattern.

THE SINKING LIFESAVER

You are beautifully set up by this individual, and when you start to sink from his sabotage, he is waiting around to pull the organization out of the situation, looking clean as a whistle. Commonly used tactics are only giving you half the story or giving you out-dated or incorrect information.

* After you have completed the test, try a different treatment with these descriptions. Instead of analyzing the people you manage in an organization, try identifying the traits of bosses and coworkers as a means of understanding how those around you operate on the job.

† Each paragraph could refer to either a male or female. Sexism in language is not intended.

THE FLOGGER

The flogger subtly and outwardly undermines everything you do. He thinks he is building you up and making himself valuable through his constant criticism. While thoughtful criticism can be healthy, this person overdoses on it, doubting everyone and questioning every decision or motive. His favorite sayings are, "I wouldn't have done it that way," "You handled that poorly," "Why are you bothering with such trivia?"

THE ROCK OF SAND

This foundation wrecker gives every indication that he is with you but usually changes his mind and never talks it over with you. Right when you need him the most, he pulls out his support and leaves you hanging. Generally, he is more concerned about with *whom* to agree than with *what*. You will find this person endorsing something, then turning around and saying that is not what he thought he was agreeing to, voting against a proposal in a staff meeting and taking the opposite view before the board.

THE WHAT MONEY?

Your fiscal officer doesn't know which side is up when it comes to the budget. Or else he does and won't tell you in hopes of covering up errors or of keeping you from controlling the money so you can't control the organization.

THE DOG IN THE MANGER

This person's self-interests outweigh those of the company or organization. Integrity of decisions, goals, or ideas brought before you are masked in selfish motives of power grabbing, monetary rewards, or successful buck passing for personal security. Beware of this sleeper!

THE OH, BY-THE-WAYER

In a voice of innocence, this person will call important matters to your attention when it is (or almost is) too late to deal adequately with the situation. The zinger is always delivered at the end of a conversation as if an afterthought: "Oh, by the way, we just discovered a half a million dollars you'll have to obligate by 5:00 p.m. today or we lose it to the Feds."

THE CELL DWELLER

The employee who used to shed light on your organization is now an honorary member of the Dark Ages. When you need it the most, the advice you get from this person is usually behind the times. He makes plans without regard to the people you serve, is out of touch with the power sources your agency needs for success, duplicates existing projects or efforts, or fouls out on projecting trends and consequences of actions.

THE PET ROCK

The office geriatrics ward is not necessarily the place you'll find this lifeless creature. He may affect to be a conqueror when in reality he is a low producer, defender against all change, and non-emitter of bright ideas. Pet rocks cost money and take up space in an organization.

THE BACK EATER

This person is hard to see because he is always acting behind your back. The creature's favorite pastime is to play forces against one another and to slander absent persons. This antagonist also likes to consider himself in charge of rumor control. The greatest danger is not in what he does to you so much as in what he continually does to upset your staff on a personal level. Cut this character's diet off before he creates any more uprisings.

LIST OF BOTHERSOME CHARACTERS

DIRECTIONS: Same as those for List of Dangerous Characters.

EXPLANATION: Once you've identified some bothersome characters, move immediately (if feasible) to resolve the problems of those who are salvageable. Frank talk, counseling, training—try what seems appropriate.

HEMORRHOID HUGHIE

He just can't sit down and do a job. He hatches good ideas, but doesn't hitch them. Hughie's never heard of charts with tasks and deadlines or of time management. It's more fun to allow constant interruptions because it makes him feel wanted. The more little errands he sets up, the more he feels "on-the-go." A good kick in the hemorrhoids will help this guy.

CHICKEN LITTLE

The sky is always falling. He sees everything as a crisis instead of a problem awaiting a solution. This character is sometimes a great benefit when giving reactions to a new proposal, but generally his constant pessimism turns into a "Sky Lab" joke.

WORDY WONDER

The only thing that would improve this source of "ear-itation" is a bad case of laryngitis. He never seems to shut up and when he says, "Do you have a minute?" he means an hour. Wordy stops by on every occasion to bend your ear and always has a bundle to say about everything.

LITTLE GENERAL

This person is so insecure with other people and his job that he hides behind a tough exterior to the point of being gruff. Rarely will you see a smile on his face or a letdown of his authoritarian veneer. No practical jokes on this one; he can't take it. If you're one of his employees, you can't help admiring him. If you don't, you're fired.

LOST AND FOUND

This person can never find those important papers when you need them. They're always around, but put away under the wrong heading or stuffed in with the extra socks in the file drawer. Lost is the kind who should never pass out papers at a meeting or the group will wait half an hour while he discovers where he put them. Sometimes your deepest wish is for this person to get lost in a department that has no Found.

CHARLIE BROWN

He's a nice guy but he lets others walk all over him. Charlie Brown is a chicken at heart and hates to try new things for fear of failure. Since he's also a self-defeater, he is amazed at himself when he performs at a high level. This fellow is most bothersome when he attends a meeting, says he did a horrible job for you (when maybe he didn't), so you never know what to make of the situation. This character requires an extraordinary amount of pep talks, but he always wants to pay you 5 cents a visit.

BARNACLE

He attaches himself to you. Have a luncheon meeting? He wants to go along. Have a special project? He wants to do it. Want a quiet cup of coffee? He wants to be there too. Also, he's so anxious to please you that he can't do anything on his own. Barnacle constantly asks if this is what you want, if this is how he should do it, to the point that it would be easier to do the task yourself than have him cling to you.

HARRY CHEST AND MS. CLEAVAGE

These two embarrass you to death. They spend more time trying to look gorgeous than they do on their work. They are also the office flirts who turn you red-faced as they seductively corner a new client, visitor, or employee before you can shoo them off. Harry Chest bothers the women with his macho "Let me do it for you," while Ms. Cleavage irks the men with her helpless "I can't possibly do that without your assistance."

MR. CLEAN

You can't just make a deal over the phone with Mr. Clean; you have to cast it in iron and have ten spotless copies on file. He spends a great deal of his and everyone else's time getting support or directions in writing in case he's ever challenged as to why he did something. If a decision he's involved in looks shaky, you can bet he has a memo on file (whether he sent it or not) advising you against the action in case it should fail and he's blamed. If he smiles when things go wrong, it's because he's thought of someone to blame.

MOUTH

This person's business is everybody's business. If you tell him something, it goes in both ears and out the mouth. His favorite introduction to a conversation is, "I'm telling you this in confidence because it was told to me in confidence." Mouth also loves to rush to friends to tell overheard news before he finds out if it's false; truth is never as exciting. You'll always find him at office parties drinking free wine, stabbing meatballs, knifing friends, and spilling the beans. Actually, he should be a train the way he runs everybody over.

COMPLAINER

This person is so bad that he would complain about the noise if opportunity knocked. He's always griping about something but would be deeply hurt if anything were done to cure the problem. His main activity is telling you how hard his job is. So when everyone is getting up to leave the office at five o'clock, he's getting up to stay . . . not out of necessity but for show. He suffers from overwork—overworking his excuses for why he can't get his job done.

LIST OF PRICELESS CHARACTERS

DIRECTIONS: Same as for other character segments.
EXPLANATION: The priceless characters are the people important to the organization's and your effectiveness. They deserve all the respect they get, whether their job is sorting the mail or supervising 1,000 people. Why note them? To make certain these people are never taken for granted, are truly appreciated, and receive tangible evidence of their value. As do

some school teachers, managers often devote more attention to the problem people than to the achievers.

EINSTEIN

This is your idea person. Somehow, he's always able to rise above the mundane and provide you with fresh new solutions. His biggest asset is being able to relate all the various facets of an organization with events in the outside business world so that his recommendations are good for the company and have some sense to them.

STITCH

Have something that needs mending? Call in Stitch; he'll fix it up in no time. He knows how to deal with difficult people and situations and is also great at taking care of all those little details that can bog down a meeting, project, negotiation session, or what have you. Stitch is also quick to bring you problems you should hear about, but always provides recommendations for you to consider for rapid action.

AU COURANT

This newshound knows what's going on. He is always up to date on the economy, business and government trends, who's in, who's out, and who's having what problems and successes in the organization. Au Courant is quick to let you in on information or people who might be helpful or useful when planning or making decisions. He also puts you in contact with stimulating individuals outside the organization and with the "diamonds in the rough" hidden throughout your operation.

THE 2,000-HOUR WONDER

These people are Mr. and Ms. Reliable, who consistently perform at or near the top of their ability. Out of the 2,000-hour work year, they are always there ready to help, even when you don't realize you need it. During those crucial moments when you need their overtime, they willingly give it but hold you to your promise not to abuse such requests. If you give them a job to do, it gets done correctly and on time. Need budget magic? They are the first to come up with the money. Tell them to take a vacation? You have to push them out the door.

BOY SCOUT

He's always prepared. This fellow is an expert in doing his homework. You can't enter a meeting without his having briefed you on the most important matters. You don't worry about his handling an important matter because he won't let a single point slip by without thorough study.

HONEST ABBY

You can trust her on anything. She's not going to lie to you or back something illegal. She keeps strategic business secrets and holds personnel problems in confidence. People like her; she means what she says and when she disagrees, it is done pleasantly and tactfully.

ZIPPER HEAD

Anytime you need information on some historical aspect of the organization, where certain records are kept on budget details, or what positions individuals inside and outside the business have taken in the past, go to him. Zipper Head has it all stored away upstairs. He's like a portable data bank that recalls anything worth remembering.

VALEDICTORIAN

He's at the top of his class, no matter what his profession is. It could be the secretary, the budget officer, the president, the janitor. Whatever the job, he is highly skilled and error free. He's so well trained in his field (even if self-taught) that you rarely have to call attention to or do any part of his job yourself. The nice thing about this person is that he knows where he's going, but won't hesitate to ask if he doesn't.

8. Tokenism in Management
A Brief Course on Beating the Rascals at Their Own Game

SHORTLY AFTER assuming your executive position, you have begun to get some not-so-subtle hints that suggest the primary reason for your appointment is your sex. It seems that the president of the corporation began referring to his yet-to-be-named top executive as "she" even before recruiting began, slips of the presidential lip that everyone remembers. And then there is the executive council—all white male, except for new you. Other senior managers sigh with relief on occasion, noting that they no longer need to respond to complaints that there is no woman in top management. When you make solid proposals, your peers smile indulgently and nod, but never make an honest assessment of what you have proposed. It seems apparent that nobody expects you to *do* anything but be present and be female.

Some of the tactics they will use to keep you in your place are similar to those listed in the chapter "The Management Leper." But there is a big difference. As their token woman, you *are* wanted, and needed, desperately.

Look at the situations in the table. Ask yourself, "Are these things happening to me?" You may wish to make your own list, placing the professional points in one column, the more personal points in another.

Column A—Professional	Column B—Personal
You are excluded from decision making.	Colleagues treat you as "cute" and "sweet."
Major developments are often not even reported to you.	Any major company problem dealing with a woman or women is automatically assigned to you.
You are not copied on key organizational memoranda.	No one at your level or above asks you to lunch, except to make a pass.
Your requests for additional staff or resources are ignored.	
No one ever really *listens* to you.	It is obvious you are being used to showcase the company's fine EEO record.
The president and other officers forget to return your calls.	

Obviously, items from Column A are more serious to you professionally than those from Column B. Take any two from Column A and add a couple from Column B and you're in trouble. You need to take action. The right kind of action is one that turns the tables on the rascals, using precisely the ammunition they have used to put you where you are.

After you have taken the following three steps, you can concentrate on solid professional accomplishment to prove your point. But first you must get all the stuff that stands between you and real success out of the way.

MANAGEMENT STRATEGIES FOR WOMEN

Step one. Recognize that they need you more than you need them. If you quit in anger and suggest that you will imply token-ism as the cause, they are in big trouble.

Step two. Become more visible. Encourage invitations to speak on your keen new management role, especially invitations from women's organizations. Local leaders of these organizations will be interested in helping. Speak at local college campuses. If you can, do a local talk show. Set up a panel on the organization's premises about women in management, inviting some biggies. Invite the in-house top dogs (male, of course). It will make them itch.

You need to build your power base where you have the inside track at the outset—among the women. Several talented women we know turned token jobs into substantive roles by *first* building such strong support among women in their industries and com-munities that The Rascals (who later reformed) *had* to take them seriously.

Step three. Demonstrate that you are a manager first, a woman second. Work night and day, if necessary, to develop loyalty and a team spirit among your staff. Plan, organize, and operate within your own shop as if you believed the top brass were totally confident in you. Give them copies of your plans and directives, asking them for comments if appropriate. While step three is an organizational effort, at the same time it is a public relations program.

NOTE: Read Niccolo Machiavelli, *The Prince.* It can be helpful.

> You must know, then, that there are two methods of fight-ing, the one by law, the other by force: the first method is that of men, the second of beasts; but as the first method is often insufficient, one must have recourse to the second.

9. What Makes a Man Really Afraid to Hire a Woman?

WE ASKED some bright, successful male executives to level with us about their fears of hiring women—the real reasons, not excuses. Knowing that failure to hire a woman *because* she is a woman is precluded by law, we promised not to share information about who said what regarding hiring!

Men cited fears of:

1. *Change* • "Our working relationship is based on friendship. Sometimes it takes that friendship to make it work. We help each other when things are tough, and we kid around to make the job fun. We just couldn't joke with women in male terms. There are still some things we wouldn't talk about with women

that we discuss as male friends." ● "Once we hire a woman for the business, we can expect our relationships with each other to change. We like the fraternity we have as men."

2. *Closeness* ● "This company is so small, bringing a woman on board will make each of us feel as if we've married her, as if we have to look out for her." ● "Sex has a lot to do with not hiring a woman professional. If you try to have the same close working relationship with a woman that you have with a man, it could lead to something else. It's *always* in the back of our minds— I've been raised to date them, not work with them! It's easier just to avoid any temptation, any complication."

3. *Feminism* ● "Professional women can be mighty militant. All of this feminism stuff can hurt an organization. It can cause problems and focus attention away from the work to be done. There are just too many women who are for the cause!"

4. *Vulnerability* ● "I can't bare my soul in front of a woman! I can't talk to her about my goals and fears about business, can't expose myself like that."

5. *Losing business* ● "It's not a matter of their [women's] competence. It's a matter of comfort for our clients. For ages the business world has been run by men. It's what our clients expect. They're used to doing business with men." ● "I can't imagine a male client telling a woman about his bad financial condition or his worries about being sued. He'll probably think: (1) 'I just can't *tell* these things to a woman,' or, (2) 'If I *did* tell her, would she be experienced enough to give me some help?' " ● "Well, we may not *lose* any business if we started hiring a lot of women, but we may not *gain* any, either!"

6. *Social pressures* ● "We just don't want to be placed in the position of having to socialize with female colleagues. Professional lives and social lives should be kept separate." ● "Because of the social stigma that is still around, we couldn't just take a woman for a drink after work or on a hunting trip and feel easy about it."

7. *Emotional and physical differences* ● "Women don't think like men. Their logic is not the same. Rules are made for men, by men. Women have to follow them. It's different, emotionally." ● "Women don't work like men. They aren't willing to put in the dirty work. They expect you to move their equipment around, lift this or that, yet they want to be treated like equals. It's easier

when we're all the same sex." • "Women want sympathy when the going gets tough. We weren't raised that way."

Not all men are afraid to hire women; we don't want to leave you with that impression. But women need to know that the fears do exist in some corners of the business world.

The critical factor in the incidence of fear is *distance*. Larger organizations with many professionals on the staff are more likely to hire women. Nobody has to get uncomfortably close to anyone else; there is maneuvering room. We found that the smaller the organization and the closer the potential male/female relationship, the greater the fear.

If you are contemplating taking a job with an organization or company you suspect is not comfortable with women in managerial roles, you have two choices:

1. Take the job (if you want and can get it), but recognize that you are on the leading edge, that there may be difficult moments, that others may resent your being there. On the other hand, it is not unreasonable to expect that your high caliber of performance *may* change things.
2. Give up the idea and take a job with a firm you know is not afraid to hire and promote women. Recognize that you may be more comfortable on the job but that you also may be trading off some business advantages for the sake of that comfort.

Our recommendation, if you choose to accept it, is the first alternative—*if* there are no other significant negatives associated with the role and the job looks terrific except for this one major problem. If everyone selects the second, change will take centuries. And we like leading edges; they rarely fail to sharpen those who try them.

10. Tips for Men. . . How to Turn Off Female Executives

THIS CHAPTER was written in response to a sincere request from a group of prestigious, highly successful male executives from around the country whom we happen to know. "Tell us," these men asked, "what it is that women are complaining about—or facing—that makes them angry! What *really* turns them off?" An answer to their question is the purpose of the following. It is *not* our aim to imply that all male executives do any or several of these things. We will say that *some* men in *some* jobs do enough of these things often enough that women are angry and frustrated and complaining. It is our feeling that the men who take the time to read the responses probably are not among those

82

who need to read them. But perhaps male readers can, through sharing the information, make good use of what follows.*

INTERRUPTING

Research† indicates that men interrupt women more than women interrupt men. Female executives are irritated and annoyed when their male colleagues jump in hook, line, and adverb because they have anticipated what the females are going to say, disagree with what they've already said, or fear what they *might* say.

APOLOGIZING

Women are distressed when, in a business situation, the men around them continually apologize for their cussing, smoking, jesting, discussing baseball, or whatever. If you really feel sorry about any of the above, don't do or say these things; if you *do* do them, don't feel sorry about it. Really, nobody cares.

BELITTLING

Do male executives *still* refer to their female associates as broads, chicks, girls, or dolls? Some do. To those few who do, we present our Tacky Toad Award, with two webbed feet.

FATHERING (NOT IN THE BIOLOGICAL SENSE)

You may be twenty years older or twenty minutes wiser, but your female colleague does not want you as her father. Fight the

---

* This is a selective group of complaints. It represents those we found most frequently voiced by female managers who have discussed their problems with us.

† Particularly, the work of sociologists Candace West and Donald Zimmerman at the University of California, Santa Barbara.

temptation to protect her, to pat her on the head, to try to take the load off her shoulders.

CATEGORIZING

Some men cannot deal with women unless they assign the relationship to convenient, comfortable, and preexisting categories. Treat her as a mother, a sister, a daughter, a favorite niece, a lover? It's not necessary. You don't have to think of your male colleagues as brothers in order to relate to them.

"X-RATED" MOVING

It happens every day. Some of you move in on women at work because you see yourselves as being romantic, because you see the women at your mercy as being receptive, because of mucho macho, because you don't know any other way to relate (see Categorizing above), and, finally, because you think you can get away with it. Nothing turns a female executive off as quickly as having you come on. Women on the way up can offer horror story after horror story; and they do, often to anybody who will listen. The practice of messing around with your female colleagues, your subordinates, and even your superiors is counterproductive, foolhardy, unsophisticated, and, ultimately, dangerous. To the men who continue to practice these tactics we present our Terribly Tacky Toad Award.

STEREOTYPING

All women are not alike, just as all men are not alike. Do you find yourself saying, "Oh, well, that's just like a woman!" If so, write 500 times, "Women want to be treated as individuals, just as men do." By the way, does your stereotypical view of women include the belief that they don't belong in the business world?

If so, don't bother writing anything 500 times. Just recognize that you are, alas, an anachronism!

PATRONIZING

Don't show favor in a condescending manner. It is insulting to the patronizer and the patronized.

IMPOSING

Everyone asks favors now and again, some more than others. The man who continually asks his female colleague to sew on his missing button, balance his checkbook, select a birthday gift for his wife, or do any one of a number of things that "women do better than men" is in big trouble with the women around him. Can you imagine, "Would you come outside and check the oil in my car?" "Will you select a present for my son for his birthday?" "Do you mind picking up my laundry? The shop is in kind of a rough part of town." How would you react to these requests from the woman in the office across the hall?

And how about imposing your manners or social values on a woman to the point of embarrassing her? Examples are fighting her to the rug over paying the luncheon check, insisting that she put out her match so that you can light her cigarette for her, scolding her for not waiting while you open the door.

BLAMING

You would be surprised at the number of men who blame the women they work with for fears that their wives have, or the men themselves have, about traveling or working closely with female colleagues.

In addition, some men blame affirmative action for keeping them in their present jobs while women and minorities "gobble up all the good jobs." It may not be a matter of affirmative action; it may be a matter of *non*-action—yours. You might not be in a better job if there were not a woman at work in the whole world!

HYPOCRITICIZING

Your paying lip service to lofty principles and not practicing what you preach—particularly with regard to fair and equal treatment for women and minorities—destroys your credibility entirely!

HIRING OUTSIDE

Hiring outside the organization is sometimes a ploy to avoid hiring the most logical in-house candidate *when* she happens to be female. And then there is the prevalent practice of hiring a male candidate of proven experience over a female candidate of outstanding promise.

ASSUMING—

- That all women have a man behind them providing financial support, which means that they do not need to earn as much income as men do.
- That your jokes about women and their alleged limitations are funny.
- That male chauvinism is a woman's problem and that *she* needs to learn to live with it or lump it.
- That all accommodations made in a male/female working relationship must be made by the female.
- That a woman is working only until she finds a mate or becomes pregnant.
- That men will not alter their own career plans to accommodate their wives' opportunities.

Tips for Men: How to Turn Off Female Executives

- That women will be content for any period of time making only minor business decisions while you make the big decisions.
- That women will not mutiny, given enough provocation. Don't count on their innate loyalty, kindness, sensitivity, turning-of-the-other-cheek, or other stereotypical traits. When enough is enough, watch out.
- That women have no real interest in your "typically masculine" topics, such as business, sports, the stock market, or, if they appear interested, that it's just for show or to impress *you*.
- That a man's work is by its nature more important than a woman's; concomitantly, that if a woman is doing the job it cannot be very important.
- That "sexual harassment" is a joke, at least when *you* practice it and it's all in fun. It is *not* a joke. It is a dehumanizing and tragic set of behaviors plaguing working relationships at all levels, management included.

11. Famous Male Putdowns and Sure-fire Replies

WHAT IS a "putdown?" The dictionary has an answer: "A dismissal or rejection, especially in the form of a critical or slighting remark."

It is important to recognize that the act of putting someone down most often is a power play; it has little to do with the subject of the putdown and everything to do with the process. The putdown is an *I'm taking control by belittling you* gambit.

Putdowners can be categorized by intent. Some, who are so eager to gain attention that they inadvertently put others down; some, who put others down as a means of putting themselves up; and others, who are highly skilled practitioners of the putdown, who use the technique to gain power and take control. It is to this last group that we will address our attention. But first, let's look at their victims—in this case, women on their way up.

Michael Korda, writing about power as the key to success for women wanting to get ahead, has some observations we think are germane to putting off those who put down.

"First of all, power is a *state of mind*—the ability to project the impression that, while others may be indecisive, confused, or weak, you know what to do, how to get it done, and have the courage, energy, and ability to do it."

Further, he says that "it is perfectly okay to *feel* weakness and doubt, but very wrong to show either."*

And one of our favorite Korda observations is, "Power is defined by other people's attitudes toward you, and, therefore, is rather like beauty—in the eyes of the beholder. . . ."

Do female managers project self-confidence? Do they display the kind of self-assurance Korda talks about? One management school experiment says they do not. From the results, we can infer that at least *some* female managers are setting themselves up to be put down.

Ross Weber of the Wharton School organized 83 four-person teams of students in management and organizational behavior courses. Sixty-two of the groups were made up of three men and one woman; twenty-one of the groups had three women and one man. Each team was assigned various business cases to analyze. For our purpose, the most interesting analyses were those each participant made of his/her position and the positions of others within their team. In the 62 male-dominated teams, half the men claimed to have been leaders and half were seen as leaders by at least one other member of their group. Among the women, only 13 percent said they were leaders; half that many were seen as leaders by any of the men.†

Is there a lesson in all of this? Indeed. Female managers need to *feel* and *display* self-confidence if they are going to be success-

* Michael Korda, "Job Power: How to Get Ahead Fast," *Harper's Bazaar,* November 1977.

† Jack Horn, "The Sexes—Being in the Minority: More Comfortable For Women Than Men," *Psychology Today,* October 1976.

ful and comfortable in their jobs. An important part of that comfort is being perceived as a competent professional, not as an amateur to be put down and rendered powerless by conversational manipulation or belittling remarks.

Self-assurance is no guarantee that a female manager *never* will receive putdowns from her male colleagues—there are always diehards. However, self-assurance *will* reduce their number and make her more effective in dealing with the rest.

Lesson one, then, is working on self. Lesson two is learning about responses to conversational bullies who use the putdown to your detriment. Let's consider three possible strategies: (1) change the subject (introduce a new topic to get the putdowner off the track), (2) terminate the conversation, (3) challenge the putdowner (this usually implies a personal challenge because the putdown remarks rarely make enough sense to allow substantive challenge).

A highly skilled practitioner of the putdown is a brilliant and talented man who holds a doctorate in psychology. The following is an actual conversation between a colleague and him. It has nothing to do with management or conflicting business situations or philosophies; it has everything to do with the process of putting down. How could the woman have handled the situation better? At what point should she have tried to change the subject, terminate the conversation, or challenge the man?

The setting is an informal gathering of top-level managers, where conversation is light and nonbusiness-oriented.

Woman: Did I tell you that I got a speeding ticket—undeserved—on my recent trip to the Midwest? Honestly, I . . .

Man: Speed limit is 55 miles per hour, Midwest, West, or East.

Woman: I know that! The point is that here I was, on this endless highway in the . . .

Man: Did you or did you not get a speeding ticket?

Woman: Well, I got a ticket, but you see what happened was that . . .

Man: Did you pay the fine?

Woman: Yes, I had to because . . .

Man: If you paid your fine, you couldn't have been very convinced that it was unfair. It wasn't smart to pay the fine. Rather dumb, actually.

Woman: But here I was, 2,000 miles from . . .

Man: Did you or did you not get a ticket? Did you or did you not pay the fine?

We leave them, the woman furious and frustrated trying to explain the circumstances whereby she received a speeding ticket she believes was undeserved and the man, cool and confident, helping her appear foolish.

Here is a business-related conversation between peers who are directors of different departments. What would have been the best way to gain control of this situation?

Woman: I cannot believe they cut $1.2 million from my budget!

Man: Why can't you believe it? It's certainly within the realm of their authority, or don't you understand that?

Woman: I understand their power! I'm just saying I cannot believe it because the program was one of the . . .

Man: Obviously they didn't think it was worth the money.

Woman: How would they know? They didn't read the information I prepared and gave them well in advance. They didn't . . .

Man: Then there must have been something wrong with your presentation. You women think all you have to do is go into the boardroom, bat your eyelashes, and get whatever you ask for. It takes a really solid presentation outlining goals and objectives, cost effectiveness, and the whole works.

Woman: I did that! All of that!

In both conversations it is apparent that the men have no interest in the substance of the discussion. Their interest lies in taking control of the conversation and in putting the woman "in her place." Questions asked of the women and superior male statements are not helpful. Note, too, the practice of interrupting. Men in these situations are far more apt to interrupt than are women. Listen to conversations around you from time to time and keep score.

An effective response to this kind of conversational bullying is total agreement—early on. The bully recognizes immediately that the agreement is a controlled response for the purpose of terminating a conversation considered fruitless. A frank gaze, a gentle smile, and "you're absolutely right" at the most unexpected time leaves the putdowner with nothing to say. It takes the power away from him. It gives you control. Once you have determined that you are in a power-play conversation with nothing to be gained, check out. Check out with calmness, style, and no rancor. "Really?" murmured in response to an insulting, outrageous statement followed by a gracious retreat is enormously effective.

What about changing the subject? Change is difficult in many cases. Putdowners are generally sticklers for hanging on to the strategy they have engineered. But it's worth a try.

And what about challenge? Challenge can be effective, given sufficient knowledge of the conversational opponent. In the speeding-ticket case, the male manager was having difficulty getting his license renewed because of several moving violations. Knowing this, the female colleague had marvelous openings for challenge.

Before challenging, remember that the "co-" in coworker means workers who act together, jointly, mutually. Therefore, any act of hostility, whether justified or not, is likely to result in further hostility, wasted time, anger, and frustration. Still, even the best managers, most skilled in the art of keeping cool, sometimes heat up. Bullies must be reckoned with, outsmarted, outscored. This is not always accomplished without unkindness or heat.

What about situations where the "co-" isn't present? Suppose the person or persons doing the frequent putting down are organizational superiors? There are four basic alternatives in this case. One is to accept the status quo, suffering mightily, and, perhaps, damaging one's self-respect. A second is fighting back, using the kinds of tactics recommended for coworkers. A third is trying to change the individual through positive, persuasive means, and a fourth is to begin a solid search for a new job.

The first alternative may be necessary for the time being, until a permanent alternative can be found. Under no circumstances would we recommend it as a long-term or even medium-term solution. The second alternative is dangerous and augurs no positive change, unless losing one's job is considered positive. The third alternative is almost an impossibility. This is not to say that all male managers of this type are not susceptible to change; it is to say that such change is slightly more likely than the sun's failing to rise tomorrow. The viable alternative, in this situation, is to look for a more positive work environment, one in which there is a healthy measure of mutual respect. One should never settle for less—for long.

Will subordinates try putting you down? Sometimes. Especially men who have not been able to overcome negative feelings about a female superior. The best defense is two-pronged: try to understand their feelings and try to help them in overcoming those feelings.

A female manager the authors know well had this experience: One of the male division heads reporting to her exhibited only polite aloofness in all of their early dealings. He was only as cooperative as he absolutely had to be to keep his job. On one occasion when they were attending an out-of-town meeting, he told her over dinner how he felt about their relationship.

"I worked for a woman once before and hated it. I've told myself I will never work for another woman. They're lousy managers. Every one of them."

She told him, "I really understand how you feel. Nearly every person I've worked for has been a male, and I've often felt at a disadvantage. It's awful to work for people when you feel their sex keeps them from giving you a fair chance."

Expecting defensive or hostile behavior from her—anything but understanding—the man was totally surprised by his manager's response. She understood and she wasn't angry! Later, when his division was confronted with a planning problem it could not solve, she came to the office and solved the problem with his senior staff. It was the barrier breaker. The next time they were on travel, he proudly introduced her to everyone as "my boss"!

MANAGEMENT STRATEGIES FOR WOMEN

Having offered sufficient warning about the dangers of lip flipping, we offer a chart of typical putdowns and some sure-fire replies contributed by those who've tried them. Have fun.

Famous Male Putdowns	Sure-fire Replies
That's not a female job!	Oh? Since when do jobs have sex?
Women just aren't any good in jobs like that! You know how they can be . . .	Yes, about 50 pounds lighter than the average man in the same job.
Isn't it difficult being a woman in a tough job like yours?	Given my biological characteristics, I have no choice.
Here, let me help you. You need a man's input.*	No, thanks. Last time I had a man's input I had an unexpected output.
You're really something! You sure don't *look* like a senior manager!	Strange. I shaved this morning.
Whatever possessed a woman like you to enter such a tough field?	Outstanding qualifications and a dozen high-priced job offers.
Listen, I really want to go to bed with you . . .	Remarkable coincidence, so does my husband (lover, next-door neighbor, uncle).
So you want to move up? What makes you think you can handle a staff of male professionals?	Oh, I think they're trainable. Even mice are.
It's really unusual to find a woman as beautiful as you who is as bright as you are!	I feel the same way about men. I've yet to find one who is really handsome and smart to boot!
How about dinner after work?	Great! I'll call my husband and the kids. They love to eat out.

* Input. Favorite buzzword in almost every organization these days. Opposite of *output* and essential ingredient in thruput. Try to avoid using all three. (See *input* and *output* in "The Woman's Glossary." Do not look for thruput. The glossary refuses to recognize the word.)

Famous Male Putdowns	Sure-fire Replies
Forgive me if my language isn't quite appropriate for a lady, but . . .	That's all right. I assume you wouldn't talk like that in front of men either, if it bothers you so much.
I'll get my girls to work on the project right away.	Aren't you afraid of child labor laws?
You really look sharp in that outfit, honeybun!	Thanks. And I intend to stay in it.
Wow! You've sure got all the beauties in your department!	Oh, so you've met Jim and Clarence?
Women are so *damned* emotional!	Calm yourself!
Who will take care of the children if they get sick?	I have a full-time houseboy.
Does your husband mind if you travel?	We have an agreement: I don't mind him, he doesn't mind me— whether we're traveling or not.

12. Zap!

ZAPPING REACHED its peak of perfection in the "Batman" television series. Missteps—taken by good fellows or bad—resulted in a lightning strike across the screen and the appearance of three big letters, Z–A–P! It was a message that missed no one. The wrong move meant a ZAP, and that was that.

We have named our management decision-making game ZAP! for what we think are obvious reasons. Make the wrong decision and, well intentioned or not, you are zapped.

Decision making is an acquired skill. It depends upon logic, inclination, organization, disposition, and a world of other characteristics. There are entire books devoted to it and courses offered in colleges for those who want to improve their decision-making abilities. Managers do not always have the opportunity

Zap!

for this kind of preparation before being thrust into situations that demand careful, thoughtful, and, most often, quick decisions. Situations may be serious, outrageous, critical, ludicrous. Still, they must be faced and resolved.

What we are asking for in this self-test are your decisions about management problems—of all kinds—that may come your way. It, too, is both serious and not so serious. Give it a try, and use the ZAP! Game Answer Key and Scoring to find your score. Then refer to Total. Learn whether you are zapless, potentially zappable, zapped, seriously zapped, or, God forbid, double-zapped. The goal is to be zapless! Select one answer.

A. You have been given so much to do that you can do nothing well. The president adds one more task.
   1. "I cannot accept this assignment until you give me additional resources."
   2. "It's an unrealistic expectation. Let's talk about it."
   3. "Sure, I can do it!"
   4. "Look! I just can't take any more! There's a limit!"
B. You have been given enormous responsibility for an area of work but no authority to ensure success in that area.
   1. Point to this obvious failure to comply with a very basic principle of good management. You may wish to share a reference from your AMA* guide or some other credible source.
   2. "I cannot accept this assignment unless I have the authority to make it work."
   3. "I have a heavy load right now, as you know, but I'll give it my best."
C. Yesterday is the deadline for completion of a difficult task you are given today.
   1. Crisis management should not be rewarded. Provide good, solid reasons why you won't drop everything and respond to an untimely, unreasonable request.
   2. Stop the shop and immediately go to work on the task.
   3. Question the need for the unreasonable deadline. If there is justification for immediate action, divert some staff resources toward getting the job done quickly and well.

* American Management Association, of course.

97

4. Complain to associates about the individual's poor planning so he, not you, gets the egg on the face if the task does not get properly completed.

D. Your travel budget is cut. You are certain the reason is to keep you from moving around enough to complete your field work successfully.

   1. "It's only half of what I need to do the job, but I certainly will do my best."

   2. "You're giving me half of what I need to do a full job. No way!"

   3. Revamp your plans. Set priorities and share them with others so that everyone will understand what work or services will be performed and what will not. Put everything in writing.

   4. Suggest diverting someone else's travel funds your way if you believe that their road show is not as critical as yours.

E. As the "person best qualified," you are asked to be Ms. Outside— to represent the organization at every insignificant meeting and conference nobody else wants to attend. You suspect this new role has been imposed to keep you from the center of activity, to keep you away from significant accomplishment, or to show off to the world that the organization has, at last, put a female in your position.

   1. Keep traveling. A moving target is harder to hit.

   2. Write memos to your boss detailing the importance of the meetings, offering suggestions about activities that could relate positively to the objectives of whatever meeting you have just attended.

   3. Send out your resume. Obviously you are not needed.

   4. Tell the boss some of these gatherings are a waste of everyone's time and ask for help in understanding why you should attend.

F. A staff member who has failed in other departments is transferred to yours without your approval.

   1. Send him packing.

   2. Privately let your good staff members know what a "zero" the new person is and not to expect much from him.

   3. With the new staff member, identify specific tasks to do for a specific period of time, ask him to set some performance goals, and at least *try* the basics of performance planning and appraisal (see "Improving Your Performance as a Performance Appraiser"). If he fails again, you will know that it is not because you have not brought the correct management principles to bear.

Zap!

4. Face the inevitable. It is a no-win situation and you know it. Level with your boss and with personnel. Leave it up to them, but let them know that you will invest no time in trying to deal with a human reclamation project.

G. Employee morale is low. As a woman, you are expected to have the kind of characteristics that are perfect to "mother" the staff and make them feel better about the organization. You are given the task of improving morale in addition to your regular work. No additional staff or funds are provided.

1. If you can do the job, regardless of sex or resources, do it. If not, be honest; say no and explain why.
2. Go ahead. Show the world that a woman can do anything.
3. Improving morale is a highly specialized task requiring appropriate professional training. If no one on staff is adequately prepared to do the job, recommend that a good consultant be brought in. Mothering won't do the trick.
4. Often just having a good listener around can make a big difference in morale. Try spending more time with those employees who are feeling down. It cannot hurt and may help.

H. A paper you wrote last month for very narrow distribution has been modified slightly, given a new title page with a colleague listed as the author, and has been widely circulated for discussion. You wonder if making a fuss about the situation will seem childish to others.

1. Demand credit when it is due you.
2. Informally recirculate the original document with a note asking, "Did you have an opportunity to comment on this paper last month? If not, I would be interested in getting your comments."
3. Confront the bastard and demand an apology.

I. Your subordinate bypasses you and gives important information to your boss which should have been reported to you. You are at a real disadvantage.

1. Give your staff a refresher course on the principles of communication. Let them know you will insist on proper reporting procedures.
2. Fire the S.O.B.
3. Let your boss know that you have some self-serving subordinates who will sink you if they can.

J. Your professional staff has given you wrong or insufficient information and has left you out on a limb.

1. Fire the lot of them.

    2. Take the time to double-check all the information the staff provides to make certain it is correct.

    3. Let your staff know your expectations with regard to accuracy. If they do not measure up, take corrective action.

K. One of your staff members, whom you have trained as your deputy, is now convinced that he can do your job better than you can. He is attempting to sink you. It is apparent he will continue to use whatever methods are necessary to make you look bad.

    1. As a competent manager you need have no fear that this man's tactics will succeed in the long run. Sooner or later he will be found out.

    2. Fire the S.O.B.

    3. You have invested time and resources in training him. Spend some more to develop new attitudes and behaviors on his part.

L. You are preparing a major report covering your total area of responsibility. You have asked for section reports from each of your division managers. It is obvious that writing reports is not their forte. The information is incomplete, poorly presented, and unacceptable for inclusion in your final document.

    1. Since the full report will go out over your signature, you had best rewrite from the table of contents to the last page. It is your fanny that is on the line.

    2. Meet with the managers and lay out for them precisely what you need and why their work is unacceptable. Let them know it is up to them to produce as requested, even though you feel certain they are incapable of doing so.

    3. Identify someone—either on the staff or in a consultant's role—who can quickly and accurately do the job. Bring that person on board to get yourself out of the situation. For the future, have your managers set some demanding performance goals for themselves and see that they get some much-needed training so they can meet those goals.

M. One of your key staff members makes a point of letting you know there was a better way to handle a situation than the way you used. He does this frequently. A lot of time is wasted debating his approach versus yours.

    1. A little disagreement is fine, but all the time? Don't debate. You're the boss.

    2. Tell your staff member to get off your case. Or, if you are comfortable with it, use more colorful language.

    3. Perhaps he is right. You had better worry about it.

    4. Fire the S.O.B.

Zap!

N. An officer-level position is open and the president of the corporation has invited you to apply for it. You know good and well he has a male manager in mind and would be uncomfortable with a female officer in his executive council. You also know that he needs to include women among the candidates he interviews.
   1. Don't ever risk your professional reputation by competing for a job you know, or strongly suspect, is a no-win situation.
   2. Increase your odds. Don't be afraid to pull whatever political strings are dangling in your direction. You may be able to force the president into giving you serious consideration.
   3. Don't play his game. Let him know you know he is trying to use you.
O. An unhealthy competition exists between two key staff members to the point where conflict is proving to be a barrier to completion of tasks in your department.
   1. Fire both S.O.B.'s if there's no hope for change.
   2. Fire the S.O.B. least likely to support you.
   3. Enlist professional help to work with your staff on building teamwork, understanding conflict, and developing communications skills. If you cannot hire someone, use your own fine talents.
   4. Competition is never unhealthy. All you must do is channel it properly.
P. A staff member, whose work is generally very good, confides to you that he is uncomfortable working for a woman.
   1. Let him know there is no place in your organization for those kinds of feelings. He will have to overcome them or get out.
   2. Appreciate his candor. Work to help him see you as a professional first and a woman second.
   3. Defend female managers as a class. Explain that they have qualities and characteristics that make them good administrators.
   4. If possible, place him under a male supervisor.
Q. An invitation to travel to an important meeting on the opposite coast has been withdrawn because the man with whom you would have to travel has an extremely jealous wife. If you go, she says, her husband cannot.
   1. Recognize and accept the fact that being female means there are some opportunities you won't have, including travel with husbands of jealous wives.
   2. Women have no business traveling away from home anyway.
   3. Discuss the situation frankly. Be firm about wanting and need-

ing to attend the meeting. Suggest that you travel alone and that you stay in a different hotel.

    4. Call the woman. Convince her that you are not interested in her husband.

R. You are delivering a speech at a meeting first thing in the morning. Tonight, your host and chairman of the meeting has invited you out for drinks and dinner. He already has remarked about your dress, your eyes (which are "magnificent"), and your style (which is also "magnificent").

    1. Go along and enjoy. Life is short.

    2. Accept the invitation in spite of warnings that there is more on this man's mind than business. Be prepared to have a fight on your hands at the end of the evening.

    3. Tomorrow is important to you and to him. Don't mess it up by getting into a compromising situation tonight. Say no.

    4. Let your feelings be your guide. If you're in the mood for a move, say yes; if not, say no.

S. Your husband is uncomfortable with your working overtime, since your staff, also working overtime, is all male.

    1. To avoid guilt feelings, don't work overtime if your husband disapproves.

    2. Help your husband recognize the true and legitimate demands of your job, which include occasional overtime hours and travel.

    3. Divorce your husband. Good jobs are more difficult to find than good husbands.

    4. Cut off your husband's allowance until he shapes up.

T. You are about to make a major presentation before your board of directors. Your secretary informs you that your child is ill. The chairman of the board is waiting impatiently for your appearance.

    1. Have your secretary get more details on the home situation immediately. How sick is the child? Can someone fill in for you at home for the period of time it will take you to make your report? Once you know the seriousness of the situation and the need for your presence, you can make a decision about dashing home.

    2. There is no question here. Go to the child as quickly as you can get there.

    3. Where illness is concerned, only Mom can help.

U. Everyone else at the meeting, where you are representing your organization, is male. Guess who is asked to take minutes? There must be a way to avoid having this happen at future meetings of this same group.

1. Rant and rave. Insist that women should not be expected to take the damned notes just because they are women. Refuse.
2. Agree to take the minutes, but make certain the final product is skimpy, inadequate, and a shabby record of the proceedings.
3. If you can use the experience to benefit yourself, do so; if not, decline with style.
4. Insist that note taking is just not one of the things you do well. Suggest someone else.

V. Because you are female, your employees keep bringing you their personal problems. You have "such a nice way of listening."
   1. Simply because you are the manager and female does not mean that you are qualified to solve your employees' personal problems. Encourage your organization to secure the services of an in-house counselor.
   2. Encourage your employees to seek outside professional help for serious problems and to leave minor problems at home.
   3. Everyone needs a shoulder once in a while. Letting your employees cry on yours is the least you can do.
   4. Seek training for yourself to improve your counseling skills.

W. You are having a bad day and are irritable. Male staff members are speculating that it must be "that time of the month." The real source of your irritation is poor staff work.
   1. Fire the S.O.B.'s.
   2. Never show irritation for fear that people will relate it to your menstrual cycle.
   3. Expressing feelings is a healthy outlet. Candor may be an asset, not a liability.
   4. When you are annoyed, deal in specifics. Let people know the problem. The staff will soon learn that your trouble relates to job performance, not sanitary napkins.

X. Because you are good-looking, and because you frequently must travel with the boss, a common misconception is that you have slept your way to your senior management post.
   1. Work full time at trying to dispel this notion.
   2. Ignore the blighters. Flaunt what you've got. They are probably jealous.
   3. Almost any action you take to change others' perceptions will work against you. Best do nothing.

ZAP! Game Answer Key

		+1	+2	−1	−2
A.	1	X			
	2		X		
	3				X
	4				X
B.	1				X
	2		X		
	3				X
C.	1			X	
	2			X	
	3		X		
	4			X	
D.	1				X
	2	X			
	3		X		
	4			X	
E.	1				X
	2	X			
	3			X	
	4		X		
F.	1			X	
	2				X
	3		X		
	4				X

		+1	+2	−1	−2
G.	1	X			
	2			X	
	3		X		
	4			X	
H.	1			X	
	2	X			
	3			X	
I.	1		X		
	2			X	
	3				X
J.	1			X	
	2				X
	3		X		
K.	1			X	
	2		X		
	3				X
L.	1			X	
	2			X	
	3		X		
M.	1		X		
	2	X			
	3				X
	4			X	

ZAP! Game Answer Key

		+1	+2	−1	−2
N.	1			X	
	2		X		
	3			X	
O.	1		X		
	2			X	
	3	X			
	4			X	
P.	1			X	
	2		X		
	3			X	
	4				X
Q.	1				X
	2				X
	3		X		
	4			X	
R.	1				X
	2				X
	3		X		
	4			X	
S.	1			X	
	2		X		
	3				X
	4				X

		+1	+2	−1	−2
T.	1		X		
	2			X	
	3				X
U.	1				X
	2			X	
	3		X		
	4	X			
V.	1	X			
	2		X		
	3			X	
	4				X
W.	1			X	
	2				X
	3	X			
	4		X		
X.	1			X	
	2			X	
	3	X			

Scoring

Refer to the ZAP! Game Answer Key. Enter on your score-sheet the number of points assigned to each answer you gave for each ZAP question.

Total

Total your points. How do you rate?

+46—zapless
+45 to +36—potentially zappable
+35 to +26—zapped
+25 to +1—seriously zapped
−1 to −53—double-zapped

13. Food for Business
The Almost-Never-Fails Take-a-Man-to-Lunch Program and Training Guide

A HIGHLY respected, successful male lawyer told us "Look. I get a lot of my new business in the restaurants and bars after hours. A female lawyer who can't or won't operate in high-class watering holes hasn't got a chance against me. I'll beat her every time."

A highly respected, successful partner in a prestigious East coast firm—this is no ambulance-chasing legal beagle. One who knows the territory, he has learned that a lot can be accomplished in a social setting.

Others, perhaps less candid or perhaps totally honest about it all, voice strong objections to mixing social life with business life. Surely there is something to be said for confining work to the business day as much as possible. But the reality is this: Whether we like it or not, approve of it or not, a lot of good business contacts and sound business relations are made and developed over lunch, dinner, drinks, or on the 18th hole.

For the career woman there are two choices—operate the way the men do or do not operate the way the men do. Of course there are levels and degrees of operation. This chapter is written expressly for the woman who has some reluctance about moving into the male-type operation; the woman who is already comfortable there does not need this training guide.

We suggest beginning with lunch. Women who do not want to be identified with the after-hours scene but who know the value of using a social setting to advantage can keep faith with their feelings and make a little professional headway at noon. If you are one of those women, we will wager that once you have mastered lunch, you will want to move on to drinks, dinner, or, perhaps, racquetball. And if your job calls for travel, you had better be able to do the evening scene as well as the aforementioned lawyer, or you may lose out.

First things first:

> It isn't evil to ask a man to have lunch, a drink, dinner, or whatever so that you can discuss a business matter. Further, it isn't evil to ask a man to do the same because you like his style or want to learn something from him.

Repeat this until you are certain you believe it.

Something else to think about is this: Whether or not *you* feel totally comfortable inviting a man for a social occasion, many men in top management today are of the generation that feels uncomfortable saying yes. Understanding that the comfort may be tenuous or one-sided at first, there are some techniques you can employ to make you both feel better about his picking up the invitation and your picking up the check.

Let's examine the two basic categories of invitees—male colleagues, and business prospects or contacts. You are apt to run into the same problems in paying the check for either category, but the invitation problems differ somewhat according to category.

INVITING

BUSINESS PROSPECTS OR CONTACTS

Trying to firm up a deal at the watering hole or on the golf course with a prospective client can create some very real problems. For many men, a female who operates in these environments is suspect from the beginning. Does she want to take him to bed? Is she after his money? Is she going to make trouble with his wife? It is outright difficult for him to realize that she wants to sell him a terrific program or product, and nothing more. If she wants to sell herself, it's her talent she's marketing, not her body. All of this seems terribly obvious, but it is not obvious at all for middle-aged, white, old-school, executive males. At least for *some* of them.

Inviting a man even to lunch under these circumstances requires some advance work—learning everything possible about his business interests, his likes and dislikes. When you approach him, let him know it is business you have on your mind. Let him know what *you* can do for *him*. Let him know you are just as talented and competent and probably more creative than Joe Hustler on the 34th floor of the Ad Building. Pique his interest. When he really begins to pay attention, ask, "How about continuing this conversation over lunch? I'd be enormously grateful if you would be my guest while we explore some possibilities . . ." No doubt he will counter with something like, "Oh, no, my dear! You must be *my* guest."

The light touch is better here. "But, please—I'm asking you! Besides, if I don't do my part in properly entertaining prospective customers, it shows on my expense voucher and I'm considered a slouch. (Sigh.) The men have *such* an advantage. People just don't reject *their* invitations."

By now he will be won over, so much so that he probably will order the mussels with garlic, fetuccini Alfredo, an expensive dessert . . .

MALE COLLEAGUES

Do a little research around lunchtime. Check the front door, and you will see the top-level male managers going out to lunch together fairly frequently. Not only do we know that the men in most organizations have their regular luncheon get-togethers but also that they have a standing poker game, handball game, or whatever. Ask them and they will tell you that these luncheons and poker-playing ploys help them in their working relationships. The officers of a prestigious Washington, D.C.–based corporation for years had the greatest floating crap game since Nathan Detroit left Damon Runyon's sewers of New York. It happened every Thursday. Unfortunately, female managers are so few and far between that they do not often have these opportunities for establishing and developing such relationships. Therefore, it is necessary to make your own opportunities. If you are a novice, stick to luncheon and dinner invitations—don't suggest poker or dice, particularly if you are good. Some people are sorry losers.

Assuming it is strictly a business occasion, stress the work-related nature of your invitation, noting the press of office demands as well as your desire to have a few relaxed moments to discuss whatever needs to be discussed. After you have suggested lunch and he agrees, inform him—casually and with confidence—that you would feel much more comfortable having him be *your* guest since you did the inviting. Do not let him interrupt as you point out how dismaying it is when *some* men (you may wish to use a slight look of disdain here) place you in an awkward and patronized position by demanding to pick up the check. It means a lot to you, you might add, to be able to ask someone to lunch—male or female—and know that he or she will be secure and confident enough to let you be your own person. Don't string it out. Don't go on and on. Don't make a big thing of it, but be quietly firm. No man, no matter how chauvinistic, can object to this rationale when it is delivered in an open, direct manner. To object, it is obvious, would be to make *you* uncomfortable.

What if there is not a solid business reason for inviting someone to dine with you? What if it is just a matter of wanting to belong, of wanting to feel more at home with your male colleagues, of wanting to get to know them better? Say so. Disarm them with your candor. They will be less fearful of the honest approach than one that is patently contrived. Do not be afraid to say, "Look, I am really impressed with the work you are doing here and want very much to learn more about it and about you. I feel rather isolated in my corner of the world right now. Could we have lunch together and get to know each other better?"

Safe? As safe as you want to make it. If, after having that first lunch you decide you like the color of his eyes better than his long-range plan for improving nonbroadcast technology, you are on your own. (See Don't kiss a frog if he's your brother, "Maxims to Operate and Succeed By.")

What if the first answer is a decided *no*? Don't assume, at the outset, that it is a putdown or that the invitee does not *ever* want to have lunch. Be confident. Be plucky. Try again.

PAYING

Chances are when the check is delivered to the table, the waiter or waitress will place it near your male guest. As unobtrusively as possible, retrieve the thing and place your credit card or cash with the bill immediately to your left (or right, depending). It helps to have your green stuff or plastic money ready early on, tucking it where you can quickly reach it when the check arrives. Digging through a handbag can be disconcerting when you are in the process of retooling a dyed-in-the-wool male chauvinist.

Plan ahead what your tip will be. Fifteen percent? Twenty? Compute quickly and be done with the check.

If, in spite of already-laid groundwork, your guest makes a grab at the check, give him a friendly stare and say, "Please. Don't make me uncomfortable."

Or, if you feel somewhat hostile about the whole thing and making a point counts more than making a friend, you might say, "Do you have a problem treating female business associates *as* business associates? Remember, I asked you to lunch, and I intend to pick up the _____ check." (Or, simply, "the check" if you do not use executive washroom language.)*

If you don't want a dispute, discretion may be the better part of luncheon valor and you may prefer to let the poor misguided soul pick up the check. He may not be worth retooling. Besides, reform is not your goal—being treated equally is. And the man who would die before letting you pay may do exactly the same thing with the men with whom he lunches; he may be treating you equally after all.

Which brings us to an important point. Courtesy, whether extended by woman to man, man to woman, man to man, or woman to woman, is a sensitive, giving commodity. In our fervor to be treated equally, each of us must recognize that treatment which is common courtesy and that which is stifling and belittling.

It is important to "feel out" your guest to learn just what distance to go at each point in the egalitarian game. You have taken control by doing the inviting, directing the conversation (see instructions that follow), and by picking up the check. That's pretty heady stuff for a lot of men. Some may need some gentling in between, such as seating you, checking your coat, and even ordering food. Mentally negotiate as you go along, creating the most positive feelings possible while maintaining the posture you have established for yourself.

---

* You can always resort to paying the check secretly on your way to the restroom; however, we prefer convincing him to tricking him.

THE 15-DAY TRAINING PROGRAM FOR AN ALMOST-NEVER-FAILS TAKE-A-MAN-TO-LUNCH EXPERIENCE

DIRECTIONS: Each step in the diagram on page 114 is keyed to the descriptions that follow. Once a step is completed, place a shiny Susan B. Anthony silver dollar on the square and move on. When the training plan is completed, you are ready to move on to Very Important Male Executives.

PART I—PREPARE YOURSELF

A. Convince *you* that you honestly want to be on an equal footing with your male colleagues. No nonsense. If you are not willing to play the game all the way, turn in your American Express card right now and forget the whole thing. If you *are* willing, pocket the card and move to B.

B. Learn how to pick up the check smoothly and comfortably. For practice, take a hungry young male to lunch several times. Generally, young men on academic scholarships, GI benefits, or working their way through college are the best source of practice material. Law students can be difficult; they may have more money to work with than other struggling students, and they almost always want to know *why* you are asking them for lunch. Within one week, select and invite two young men to lunch.

C. Plan a conversation strategy and test it. *You* determine what the discussion will focus on, how it will develop, and when. Outline what it is you want to result from that discussion, look your guest in the eye, and kindly, but firmly, lead him to where you want him to be.

PART II—PREPARE HIM

A. Issue an invitation to lunch.

B. Through your confident attitude, let the man know you feel

MANAGEMENT STRATEGIES FOR WOMEN

comfortable about being the taker rather than the takee. Give him time to become accustomed to the idea.

C. Give him something to think about during the interval between invitation and lunch (you should allow two or three days). Introduce a topic or an idea you want to discuss later, over the caesar salad.

PART III—CLOSE WITH STYLE

It is assumed that your luncheon invitation was extended and accepted courteously. It is also assumed that you and your guest got to the restaurant feeling relaxed and comfortable. The discussion went well. When it is time to part, there could be awkward moments. He is not accustomed to thanking *you.* And who suggests what with regard to the next time you meet?

A. Thank *him* first. "Thanks for coming along. I really appreciated your being so supportive . . ."

B. When he returns the thanks, a warm smile and nod will do. If there is an inspiration to make a remark justifying your having invited him, stifle it. The more casual the better.*

C. He will probably say, "Next time, it's my treat." If he does, accept with grace—if you wish. If he doesn't suggest a next time and you wish to, you might say something like, "I hope we have other opportunities to get together informally. I enjoyed it."

---

* If you catch yourself saying, "Gosh, I hope it was all right to suggest lunch," go back to square one, remove Ms. Anthony, and start over.

14. The Planning Mystique
Charting the Course; Making the Voyage

It is our belief that the difference between an average manager and a great manager most often lies in the planning and organizational abilities of the individual. People who reach the top, and who stay there, generally know where they want to go and how to get there before they begin rising. The same thing is true for organizations.

Planning is a highly specialized discipline. It is our purpose here to introduce some basics about that discipline that can be especially helpful. In doing so, we have attempted to break planning down into reasonable parts, starting with the planning course and ending with the actual voyage.

Because planning is a highly specialized discipline and covers many elements by many names, we do not expect that you will become great planners in one easy lesson. Instead, we hope to help you become knowledgeable about what planning is, what the various characteristics of planning are, and how you might expect to fit into the overall planning function in your organization. Further, we have included a helpful interview with a great planner, Dr. John Rockart of the Sloan School of Management, who offers sound advice about the topic. We include a list of situations that can lead to planning mutiny, also the Great Planning Voyage from Here to There—a game, of sorts.

CHARTING THE COURSE

Planning is one of the most basic of all managerial roles. It helps the manager chart the future of the organization and the part everyone will play in the days, months, and years ahead. If the chart is clearly understood and soundly structured, employees will comprehend what is expected of them, what they are to accomplish as part of a group, and toward what end their group work is directed.

Unless there is planning, the future course of an organization is left to chance. Unfortunately, few companies can afford to risk survival in a complex era of fluctuating economy, an uncertain money market, changing social or political demands, and rapid development of technology. Therefore, more and more organizations are trying to minimize risk* and take better advantage of opportunities through the demanding but important process of planning.

Since planning for a *total* organization is a relatively new phenomenon and still a challenging one for many managers, the purpose of this chapter is to take some of the mystique out of planning and to offer some suggestions concerning a leader's first steps.

What *is* planning? Essentially, it is the process of (1) establishing goals and objectives for an entity and the separate organiza-

* Or, as Peter Drucker says, to expose the risks so that one can make more intelligent decisions.

tional units within that entity; (2) establishing policies, methods, and strategies to guide work toward the achievement of goals and objectives; (3) assessing and allocating resources necessary to implement strategies; and (4) establishing mechanisms to control and evaluate progress toward goal achievement. (We believe planning and control are indivisibly linked and therefore have included control as part of our planning cycle.)

The following can be used as a framework to assist managers in identifying the kind of planning they want and need to do. We believe the key to achieving desired results in a company begins with a manager's ability to (1) see how her area of responsibility fits into the whole planning picture and (2) tell her workers the characteristics she wants in a plan.

CHARACTERISTICS OF PLANNING

Over the last few years, managers have been exposed to (and sometimes bewildered by) a multitude of planning processes and systems. They include zero-based budgeting, management by objectives, planning/programming/budgeting, results-oriented management, and more. There are also program plans, policy plans, comprehensive plans, master plans, organizational plans, strategic plans, long-range plans, short-range plans—the list goes on. Many a manager has gotten lost in the vocabulary.

To avoid getting waylaid by the terminology, let's look first at the characteristics of planning—the fundamentals of what planning *does.*

In the table on pages 120–21, we have outlined three categories of principal planning characteristics. The format is intended to help one differentiate between the various levels of planning that can take place within an organization.

YOUR ROLE IN THE PLANNING PROCESS

There are plans for various periods of time, various areas of responsibility, and various purposes. Ideally, plans for day-today, month-to-month, and year-to-year activities or strategies should all mesh so that short-range decisions contribute to and do not hamper long-range desires and commitments.

Furthermore, a single area of an organization may do one or several types of planning. Some set broad goals, some determine broad steps to meet those goals, some outline specific and measurable tasks that eventually will lead toward goal achievement. Some might work on all three levels. Ideally, again, what one group is planning should not conflict with the plans of another area or the overall corporate activity or organizational aims.

We suggest, then, that a manager might want to view the planning process as a matrix of sorts. Within this matrix (or grid) is a time factor, a "turf" factor, and a level-of-planning factor. The entire grid represents all the plans being formulated in the organization.

Each manager should try to locate her space in the matrix by asking these questions:

1. For what areas of the organization am I to plan?
2. What level of planning is appropriate for each of my areas? General, specific, or somewhere in between?
3. For what period of time do I plan for which area?
4. How will all my plans fit in with those of the entire organization?

A FOOTNOTE TO CHARTING THE COURSE

Does this mean that once all these plans are made, one forgets planning and skims along at full sail until the globe is circled? Not at all. One must recognize that the activity is dynamic and evolving and should be willing to modify course, allocation of resources, and even goals—if there is reason to do so. If a hurricane is building along the planned course, you had best change course; don't expect the hurricane to change its course for you.

Principal Characteristics of Goal Setting	Principal Characteristics of Goal Reaching	Principal Characteristics of Assuring Goal Attainment
Answers the basic questions: "Why are we here? Where do we want to be in the future? What are our basic strategies and goals to guide the organization toward our future role? How much money do we have and how shall we spend it to do what we want to do?"	Answers the basic questions: "What steps shall each unit take to reach company goals? Will these steps mesh with overall corporate strategy? What human and fiscal resources are needed to do the job?"	Answers the questions: "How can we assure that tasks are being carried out efficiently and effectively? How will we know when corporate and unit goals and objectives are met? How much of our resources have we spent and how well?"
Looks at the future. Opportunities for and potential threats to the organization are forecasted. Broad strategies are determined to make certain the company will adapt and thrive in the future.	Determines steps (usually called objectives) to meet corporate and unit goals.	Determines precise statements that describe expected results in quantitative terms accompanied by exact deadlines for each program, activity, or project within a major unit.
Sets broad goals for the organization. These are statements of long-term intent specifying the overall aims and purposes of the business.	Revalidates or redesigns company programs and product lines in accordance with corporate strategy and the above objectives.	Sets up procedures for measuring progress toward desired results and corporate goals.
Sets narrower goals for each major unit in a company. They mesh with broad company goals.	Outlines what human and fiscal resources are needed to meet specific objectives.	Sets up procedures to control the effective and efficient use of material and fiscal resources.
	Outlines specific responsibilities for each unit or subunit within the planning scope.	Sets up procedures to measure, appraise, and improve workers' efficiency.

Sets broad policy for company operation toward goals.

Sets up the organizational structure.

Assesses and allocates fiscal resources in accordance with overall company goals.

Establishes broad time frames and evaluation/measurement policies for work to be accomplished.

Sets up procedures for hiring, promoting, demoting, and dismissing personnel.

The total often leads to plans called (for example):

Strategic Plans
Long-Range Plans
Structural Plans
Master Strategy

The total often leads to plans called (for example):

Departmental Plans
Divisional Plans
Long-Range Plans
3–5-Year Plans
Long-Term Project Plans
Organizational Plans
Operational Plans
Budget Plans

The total often leads to plans called (for example):

Short-Range Plans
Administrative Plans
Short-Term Project Plans
Program Plans
Task-Development Plans

The sum total often leads to plans called (for example):

Comprehensive Plans
Master Plans

121

MAKING THE VOYAGE

There are some very practical matters that should be taken into consideration whenever a manager embarks on a planning project.

First of all, she should be aware of common mistakes or pitfalls that can make planning go wrong in an organization. She will want to avoid falling into the planning "drink." For an interesting view on this point, we met with John Rockart, director of the Center for Information Systems Research of the Sloan School of Management at the Massachusetts Institute of Technology. He specializes in management information systems, planning, and control. The man is practical. That's why we interviewed him.

When asked what he felt were the most significant reasons an organization finds itself with planning troubles, he listed four.

1. *Neglecting strategy, neglecting strategic planning.** Why is that bad? "Because you wind up continuing to do better and better in what you already do, when the environment is changing so quickly that you may have to change essentially *what* you do."
2. *Just planning without implementing.* "You can spend an awful lot of time figuring out what to do. The hard part is setting up the mechanism for a manager by which she is sure that the plans get carried out."
3. *Believing that you ought to carry out the plan as it was written several months or several years ago.* "The environment changes. Plans have to be adjusted to things you weren't smart enough to see

* Strategic planning as used here refers to our column of planning characteristics headed Goal Setting. He defines strategic planning as "the process of looking at the environment of the future and looking at the organization of today. A manager analyzes the strengths and weaknesses of her business and asks what opportunities the environment of the future is going to offer, what threats it imposes, and then revalidates or redesigns the organization's programs, activities, or product lines to make sure the company thrives in the future."

were going to happen." However, this statement should not provide someone with the excuse not to follow through. "That's the reason that management is an art and run by people and not by computers. The good executive knows when to press like hell to make sure the plan is carried out and knows when to be willing to scrap a previous plan and replan."

4. *Having a planning process which is essentially run by a planning officer, without heavy line involvement in the planning process.* "Good planning has top line* involvement and extensive planning staff help. Either line or staff doing it alone is a mistake, but planning staff alone is the biggest error. Since planning is the first part of a planning-*control* cycle, line executives *must* be involved if this year's efforts are to be carried out." Staff help is also needed, however. "It helps to have some people to whom they can assign the function of getting the planning process finished and of gathering additional data as necessary."

The second practical matter that managers might wish to review is the difference between planning *theory* and actual *practice.* The review may help one take a more practical view of planning processes, opportunities, and limitations. Since Dr. Rockart serves on the board of directors of two corporations and consults and teaches for several major companies, we asked for his views about the slips between theory and practice.

According to Rockart:

- *Most organizations cannot plan by the textbook.* "Some of the major leadership companies that are huge can afford to do it the way the textbooks outline it, because the textbooks really are written with them in mind. There are a lot of other organizations under the gun that really *have* to tailor the planning process to themselves and their executives. I also know of organizations that have executives who will not sit down and plan. They just work like hell. They get insights, they scan the environment, and they change the organization a little bit. Somehow, in many situations, that works very well, mostly in smaller organizations. The major thing is that the planning process must fit the particular organi-

---

* Rockart says, "Both planning and implementation are line functions. The person in charge of that part of the organization (or the entire organization) where the plan was developed has got to be the person to carry it out."

zation, its environment, the capabilities and desires of the chief executive, and the amount of threat the organization is currently under."

- *Few organizations carry out all phases of planning according to theory. There isn't the correct environment, planning organization, or the time for it.* "Planning takes time away from the present. Most managers are going to try to do a minimal amount of it with a minimal effort. Frankly, that's one of the reasons why strategic planning isn't being done as much as it should be. I've found, however, that the strategic planning process can be tailored to fit situations which appear quite different each time I work with an organization."

- *Theory says to involve everyone concerned in the planning process; practice may be very different, but for some good reasons.* This seems to be occurring chiefly among presidents of smaller companies and some managers in the public service area. As Rockart explains it, perhaps these individuals have come to believe that their organizations will never get off the ground if they have a "you-all-come" and "everybody-gets-to-approve," time-consuming planning process.

"Alternatively, some believe that a formal strategic planning process (given the orientation of their particular executives) will lead to huge disputation, bickering, or the inflexible setting of a course into the past. Therefore, some of these managers have elected to take a different leadership role: they develop the planning strategy informally and either announce the direction toward which everyone is expected to head or, more subtly, guide, encourage, and coax the personnel in their organization in the right strategic direction."

THE GREAT PLANNING VOYAGE FROM HERE TO THERE

Planning is serious business. We do not intend to imply otherwise in taking a light approach with our Great Planning Voyage. Rather, the intent is to have some fun with the planning process and, at the same time, to provide something of a review of things to do and not to do in getting from here to there in a plan. Read each statement, and if you agree, follow the italicized instruc-

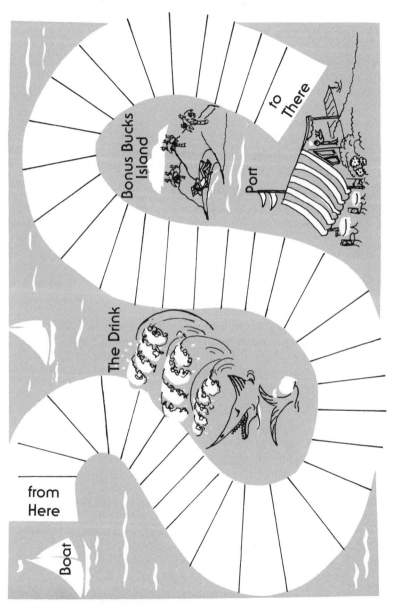

tions which apply to the "game board." Use a good-luck charm to mark your progress along the course.

1. Review broad goals and strategies of the organization. *Hoist anchor. Go ahead two.*
2. Define the purpose of your program in the context of existing plans. *Go ahead three.*
3. Your statement of purpose should reflect only your own ideas. Isn't that why they hired you? *Go back one.*
4. Never think about the future. Never stop to ask, "Why do we do it this way?" "Should we be doing this?" *Mutiny!*
5. Establish specific objectives that mesh with organizational goals. *Go ahead two; side trip to Bonus Bucks Island.*
6. Make your objectives reflect the independent, visionary nature of your department *only*. Don't pay attention to the direction the rest of the organization is going—they probably don't know what they're doing anyway. *Drop anchor until you understand the synergetic nature of planning!*
7. The crew is making goals and objectives fit *their* interests rather than those of the organization. Install an early warning detection device to avoid this problem. *Go ahead one.*
8. Some enchanting Siren singing on a rock off the starboard bow is attempting to lure you off course with wily suggestions that you really believe are doomed to failure, "sexy" though they may be. Stuff wax in your ears. It worked for Odysseus. *Go ahead four. Remove wax.*
9. Develop great strategies to meet future opportunities and threats. In doing so, use *all* research and analytical tools available and appropriate. *Go ahead two; side trip to Bonus Bucks Island.*
10. Hire your best friend to come up with an idea to solve a planning problem that is plaguing you. *Go directly to the Drink.*
11. Identify resource needs—fiscal, human, special services. *Go ahead two.*
12. Prepare budget with utmost care and meticulous detail. *Go ahead three.*
13. Do some creative budget padding. Don't cheat; just give yourself some maneuvering room. *Go ahead one.*
14. No need to worry about finances. The tooth fairy loves female managers. *Are you kidding? Go back three.*
15. Don't involve the power sources in your planning. They may not fire a shot across your bow. *Go directly to the Drink.*

16. Plan allocation of human resources. Define responsibilities. Include performance standards. *Go ahead two.*
17. Employees complain that their supervisors did not allow them to participate in setting their performance standards. Since you realize that employees normally will set higher standards for themselves than their supervisors will, you insist the process be redone and include employees. *Go ahead two; you are very wise.*
18. Design administrative control procedures for program. *Go ahead two.*
19. Don't be concerned about programmatic controls; fiscal controls are really all that matter. *Go back two.*
20. The budget officer complains that your fiscal projections are not realistic. Go over his head to the vice president. *Go directly to the Drink.*
21. Use persuasive communication and negotiation to reach agreement on your budget. *Go ahead two; side trip to Bonus Bucks Island.*
22. Keep yourself so totally involved with the planning function that you forget to manage the day-to-day activities for which you are responsible. *Mutiny!*
23. No one involved with planning seems to know to whom they should report during the process. Redefine reporting responsibilities and ask each individual to provide you with a statement which details their understanding of your instructions. *Go ahead one.*
24. Determine evaluation criteria. Know how you are going to measure results. *Go ahead two.*
25. Design both ongoing and end-product evaluation procedures. *Go ahead two.*
26. Who's counting? Do not plan to measure activities against plans or expenditures against budget. If things go wrong, it's harder to tell. *Go back to start.*
27. Although your plan calls for a final printed report, there is no budget item for printing costs. Don't be concerned. The budget officer is picky-picky about a lot of things. *Go back two.*
28. Focus on crises. With a little effort you can become a crisis-oriented manager who doesn't need to spend any more time planning. *Go directly to the Drink.*
29. The budget comes back again. You forgot to include employee taxes and benefits in figuring salary costs. Resubmit it; someone else can do those kinds of details. *Tsk, tsk. Go back one.*
30. It seems that the work underway can never be accomplished by your present staff. Since planning is of an ongoing nature, you

pare your needs as much as possible and seek additional permanent, well-qualified help. *Go ahead two.*

31. Don't worry about more work than your staff can handle. There's always temporary help. *Go back two.*

32. A member of the board insists that you change one of the strategies in your one-year plan; his insomniac mother dreamed up a better idea. You agree to the change. *Go directly to the Drink.*

33. You suggest that the mother of the board member drink warm milk before retiring; you hang on to your strategy. *Go ahead two.*

34. Keep in mind that you must spend *every penny* budgeted or you might not get what you request next time around! *Go back two.*

35. Test planned activities and procedures against existing plans and policies to ensure that they mesh. *Go ahead two; stop by Bonus Bucks Island.*

36. Once plan is complete and in good form, distribute to appropriate individuals and units for reaction and response. Make those modifications that will enhance the program, increase its value in terms of overall goals and objectives, and not exceed available resources. *Go directly to Port! Voyage complete.*

15. Avoiding Tooth-Fairy Economics

YES, VIRGINIA, it's true. There is no tooth fairy. No good elf leaves money under the pillow or on the stump to bail out floundering businesses or mismanaging managers. And worse, there is nothing sprouting in the budget vineyard that looks like a money tree. Managing money, at any time, is serious business; it is *very* serious business in times of rising inflation and recession indicators. All of this means that even non-financial managers had better know as much as possible about the economics both of the day and of their particular business. If they do not, they might as well believe in tooth fairies and money trees.

Given the absence of elves and magic trees, how does a skillful manager, not trained in financial management per se,* improve her chances for success and diminish her chances for financial misfortune?

She does a number of things. We have listed eight which we think are extremely important. They operate on three levels: departmental, organizational, national. We do not intend to suggest that a woman must be a financial whiz kid; rather, that she should be knowledgeable about financial planning and management in her own organization and about the economic context in which that organization will succeed or fail.

EVALUATING YOUR FINANCIAL KNOWLEDGE

To test your understanding of what's what on the money side of management, score your knowledge against each of the following. Give yourself 5 points for good understanding or experience and 0 for no knowledge, with adequate understanding or experience rated at 3. Look at the skillful nonfinancial manager and at *you*

1. *She* understands the source of funding or income which supports her organization or company. In the business world there are two types of sources: capital—intended for investment—and revenue—income from the sale of products or services. Capital can come from stockholders, who invest their money and thus have an equity, or ownership, in the business. Capital also can come from borrowed money.

   In the nonprofit sector, funds may come from public monies

* In reviewing hundreds of applications for senior management positions (some in the $50,000-and-up category), we have noted that women often lack the financial management skills or knowledge of their male competitors. It is our belief that women, sometimes thrust into management when the company decides it needs some competent women "up front," have not had sufficient opportunity to prepare for this area of management. Men, aiming for the top from the very beginning, make certain they gain the necessary background to compete at every step along the way. Such is not always the case, but experience with women job seekers prompts us to express concern and to encourage women to gain experience and understanding in financial management.

dispensed through various government entities or from private sources such as foundations, endowments, individuals, and the like.

Whether the source of money is public or private, it is important to learn as much as possible about the source or sources that are the power behind the company throne. This knowledge helps in understanding the range of fiscal possibilities and limitations that exist in one's own realm; it helps in understanding budgetary decisions.

What are the sources of income for *your* organization or company? What percentage is derived from which source?

Score _____ (0, no knowledge; 5, full knowledge)

2. *She* is knowledgeable about the company's or organization's fiscal policies and procedures. This includes knowing who has what authority to make which fiscal decisions; which programs, projects, or products receive priority monetary support; whether discretionary monies are set aside for "targets of opportunity" or bail-outs; what company policies are with regard to investment and return; and a world of other financial facts.

Can you describe *your* company's or organization's *principal* fiscal policies or philosophy that guide(s) funding decisions for your area of activity?

Score _____ (0, no; 5, yes)

3. *She* knows how to prepare a departmental budget that is correct in form and figures, comprehensive in content, and consistent with company and departmental goals and objectives. This means that she works with correct *assumptions* (see Planning, which follows) in preparing her budget. It means that she has used every opportunity to express her plans and intentions through the unique eloquence of numbers. She never makes a budget presentation with ideas only half thought out; her budget expresses the thoroughness of her plans and her knowledge of how best to implement them.

Can *you* prepare and present a budget for your department?

Score _____ (0, no; 5, yes)

4. *She* understands the real world of the budget-request/budget-approval process and how to use it to her advantage. Not everything one asks for is funded; too, those projects and operations funded may be cut arbitrarily by the budget authority to a level far lower than that requested. Knowing this, she does a little creative padding and fattening. And she uses *negotiation* (see "The Woman's Glossary") to reach a compromise that is really a win, instead.

Do *you* know how to use your internal budget-approval process to your advantage? Do you know how to get what you want (within reason, of course)?

Score _____ (0, no; 5, yes)

5. *She* has a reputation for sound management of her budget. There were few budget variances, no sloppy overruns, no financial problems last year or in previous years. She expended funds as planned and achieved, for the most part, the results as promised. Budget decision makers trust her.

What was *your* track record last year for management of your budget? Were variances few or nonexistent?

Score _____ (0, major problems; 5, no problems)

6. *She* is knowledgeable about her organization's or company's current and historical financial positions. She can answer such questions as these: What has been the organization's financial growth pattern? What kind of return has it provided for investors? Has there been readily available working capital to take care of increasing inventory needs? If it is a nonprofit organization funded by the government, have appropriations traditionally been held up by tacked-on, irrelevant amendments? Has financial stability been rocked by *continuing resolutions** at

* Interim funding pending approval of coming year's budget.

the beginning of the fiscal year and windfalls at the end? And what about today's financial position? Tomorrow's? Where do we stand?

What has been *your* organization's financial position over the past few years? How does it stand today?

Score _____ (0, no knowledge; 5, very knowledgeable)

7. *She* is at least familiar with the basics of accounting. This does not mean that she is a CPA or genius at cost accounting. It does mean that she will know whether certain costs connected with her division's manufacture of the new disco widget should be charged against operating costs or costs of sales. It means that she will understand how books are kept and be familiar with basic accounting principles and terms.

Do *you* know the accounting basics? Do you know how your company keeps track of fiscal activity?

Score _____ (0, no knowledge; 5, very knowledgeable)

8. *She* reads the *Wall Street Journal, Fortune,* or other publications that provide a reliable picture of general economic trends and important business news. It is almost impossible to understand fully the financial opportunities and problems of an organization without understanding something of the ever-changing economic context within which that organization is operating.

Do *you* read the *Wall Street Journal, Fortune,* or other publications that give reliable information on economic trends and business news?

Score _____ (0, never; 5, regularly)

Scoring

Each question included in this self-test should be considered separately in terms of scoring. Any answer that does not score 3 or above means attention must be paid to that particular area. Correction or improvement is indicated.

The tooth fairy does not come to female managers; therefore, knowledge must.

BUDGETING

Managers will be most directly involved with *operational budgets* for their own areas of activity, and it is on this kind of budget that our discussion will focus. However, managers should at least be familiar with other kinds of budgets which their organizations may use. There is the *capital budget*—the company's plans for purchase of capital assets—and the *discretionary budget* —usually the political cookie jar from which treats may or may not be dispensed according to the merit of requests.

In the profit-making sector, and sometimes in the public sector, managers may use a monthly *cash budget* to forecast profits and losses. These budgets allow a manager to plan for contingencies rather than to be at their mercy. They allow a manager to see clearly how fluctuations in a given market can be expected to affect her operation. She then can determine when to correct, by how much, and for how long. This is extremely helpful in small businesses where *cash flow*, the amount of actual cash made available by business operations, is often a problem.

Organizations may have other budgets, but these are the most interesting and most relevant for nonfinancial managers.

There are three principal objectives of financial budgeting: (1) *planning*, which amounts to expressing in dollars and cents the level and scope of activity anticipated over the budget period; (2) *coordinating*, or balancing the financial plans of all units within the organization to ensure responsible and realistic operation; and (3) *controlling*, or comparing expenditures against plans as the period and activities progress or end.

Most managers will have direct responsibilities with regard to two of these activities—planning and controlling. Coordinating usually involves managers in a game-show event called Run for the Money. In this game, program managers compete with each other to win the heart and allocations of the budget officer or public appropriations body (there are those who claim budget officers and their public-sector equivalents have no heart, which may explain why the game is so difficult). Traditionally, program managers ask for much more money than they expect to get (see point 4, Evaluating Your Financial Knowledge). The budget decision makers understand this ploy and recognize their duty to cut requests. The skill of asking for enough excess to allow for the cut is highly developed in some managers.

PLANNING

In planning her operating budget, a manager must have before her certain common *assumptions* on which to base her request. She must know, for example, that the company plans a 7 percent across-the-board salary increase next year before she can determine her staff costs. She needs to know if the decision has been made to limit consultants' fees to 90 percent of those of last year. She must know the level of services her company intends to provide in the coming year.

Essentially, the manager's role is to translate into dollars and cents the plans she has made for her unit's activity during the budget period and within a framework of prescribed assumptions. She will indicate staff and support costs, equipment and service costs, special project costs. If she is in charge of the new disco widget, she will have, in dollars and cents, a description of what she will have produced by year's end and at what cost. Her expenses will be line items, detailed by category.

Under certain circumstances, her operating budget may be a *flexible budget,* which is a whole set of budgets based on the same organizational assumptions but with a variable. This kind of budget says, "This is what we will do *if*. . . ." If the market fluctuates, Budget A may be replaced by B or C to fit the new economic circumstances. Flexible budgets are much easier to live with, generally speaking, than are inflexible budgets.

135

Another form of operating budget is the *program budget,* often used in the not-for-profit sector. It may be called by any one of a number of names—PPBS (planning/programming/budgeting system), ZBB (zero-based budgeting), or XYZ (you name it). Whatever it is called, it is a system of budgeting that goes beyond describing and categorizing departmental expenses. It requires justification for costs in terms of overall benefits and specific objectives achieved. Analyses focus on results that are not written in the common language of dollars and cents, but rather in terms of social benefits.

CONTROLLING

A difference between plans and expenditures, whether in the public or private sector and whether one is using a traditional or program operating budget, is called a *variance.* Not all variances are negative. For example, there may be greater sales at less cost than anticipated. However, the name of the budget-control game generally is to reduce or eliminate variances.

In the nonprofit sector, variance often sparks a phenomenon which we can describe as end-of-the-fiscal-year creative spending. Agencies or departments that have not had the level of expense anticipated, rush to make last-minute expenditures. They do so to avoid returning funds to the source, which will then put them on another department's stump or under its pillow. In addition, the source does not forget underspenders. It reduces their level of spending for the next year.

The seriousness of budget overruns depends upon where you are operating and for what purpose. If the purpose is profit-making, you may be in big trouble. If the purpose is public service, the overrun may be compensated for by transferring funds from one department or service to another, which may or may not be serious depending upon the organization's plans and accomplishments.

ACCOUNTING

A budget puts plans into action. Accounting keeps track of that action. It uses the common language we have been discussing—dollars and cents. The difficulty with the language, which becomes most apparent with accountants' reports, is that it can be misinterpreted. For one thing, bottom lines, which show net income after taxes, do not necessarily show available money. And today's balance sheet might indicate that your company is in a terrific position, but that balance sheet reflects your position at a single point in time. Events that will take place next week, which do not show on the balance sheet, may affect your position significantly. Further, some of your assets may be in the form of accounts receivable that you will never collect, or your delivery trucks may be on their last wheels. Your inventory may be so obsolete that the value listed on the balance sheet is enormously inflated. On the other hand, you may own assets of far greater value than indicated. Your building, purchased 10 years ago has increased significantly in value. While you can show the negative changes (depreciation) for some of your assets, you do not show positive changes. You do not indicate that your real estate investment has quadrupled in value.

All of this is by way of saying that the language of accounting is money, but that it speaks with complex tongue. Managers new to the language should not jump to conclusions when they see the balances in the balance sheet or the bottom lines in the income statement. It takes careful and thorough examination of all available financial data to get a clear picture of what is what. And then the picture probably will require an accountant to get it into fine focus.

Companies use both the balance sheet and the income statement to measure their performance. Other indices are used, among them the *return* measurements. How much return is there for how much investment or use of assets? The answer has much to do with the company's overall health and well-being.

Briefly, among the measurements are: return on investment (ROI), return on invested capital (ROIC), return on equity (ROE), and return on assets used (ROAU).

It is not possible, in the context of our discussion of tooth fairies, to wave a magic wand and provide immediate knowledge of the intricacies of accounting procedures. It is possible to recommend a couple of excellent books which we think are particularly helpful.* We also are suggesting a learning outline, below, to guide you to what you *really* need to know about accounting to function effectively as a nonfinancial manager.

1. Learn to analyze a balance sheet. Understand the basic terms, where they belong on the balance sheet, and *why*.
2. Understand why a balance sheet *always* must balance.
3. Understand what a balance sheet can tell you and what it cannot. Why do you need analyses other than the balance sheet before deciding to purchase or make a major investment in a business?
4. Understand the nature, content, and purpose of the income statement. What does it tell you that the balance sheet does not?
5. Learn which kinds of business transactions are reflected in the balance sheet and which in the income statement.
6. Set up an imaginary company. Draft a balance sheet for your new creation, listing all assets (current and long-term), all liabilities (current and long-term), and all capital/equity. Have your "company" incur costs of sales and operating costs, and pay taxes. Have it make sales. Develop an income statement to tell you how well your company is doing.

---

* Robert N. Anthony, *Essentials of Accounting* (Reading, Mass.: Addison-Wesley Publishing Co., 1976), a workbook programmed by Matthew L. Israel, 2d ed.; Robert Follett, *How to Keep Score in Business* (Chicago: Follett Publishing Co., 1978).

16. Improving Your Performance as a Performance Appraiser

IF DEATH and taxes are certainties, so also is performance appraisal in the life of today's manager. It may happen every spring or every fall, but rest assured it will happen at least once a year. When the season arrives, welcome it. Before it arrives, prepare for it.

A sound performance evaluation system can be one of your most effective management tools. It can help you identify those employees ready for advancement and those ready for an exit interview. It can reveal beginning problems which can be resolved easily with some immediate attention. And, if you are able to deal with evaluation of your own performance, it also can tell you something about your effectiveness as a manager.

In the following pages, we have described our favorite performance planning, review, and appraisal methodology and have provided a practice exercise for those who are seeking a new system.

Basically, we find three major obstacles to effective performance evaluation: (1) the desire on the part of managers to be liked by their employees; (2) fear of grievances or lawsuits if evaluations are not positive enough; and (3) a general trend, especially in governmental agencies, to encourage mediocre performance through policies which discourage either outstanding or unsatisfactory ratings.

Even the toughest manager, whether he or she admits it, prefers to be liked rather than disliked by employees. This is reasonable, given that most of us are more comfortable in a friendly atmosphere, one conducive to supportive behavior and attitudes. And once an employee is told he or she is not measuring up, the atmosphere *can* change in a hurry. In today's world of work, minimum-wage employees as well as senior staff members may threaten to file legal actions or in-house grievances if they believe their performance evaluations are unfair. With no agreed-upon measurements on which to base a judgement about performance, opinions of what is unfair can vary from one extreme to the other. A super-grade Federal manager told us that if he were to evaluate a poor performer honestly and objectively, he would have to take "a solid year away from the desk to fight the union." Other managers, not in government, say it "just isn't worth the time and money" to fight suits and grievances brought about through honest performance evaluation.

Finally, many organizations—inside and outside government circles—really *do* encourage mediocre performance. If a manager rates an employee *outstanding,* she must complete an extensive justification of the evaluation. If the same manager rates an employee as less than *good* (even *satisfactory* is considered by many to be an unacceptable evaluation), a similar paperwork exercise is mandated. The only way to move quickly and smoothly through performance evaluation in these instances is to rate everyone the same—something between *good* and *very good.* Once employees realize that average is the name of the performance game, that may be the level of their performance.

What about women? Do they have special problems?

Performance appraisal *is* a tough area, perhaps the toughest. And if anything flies in the face of the most typical of all stereotypes—that of the gentle, forgiving, and understanding female —it is the act and fact of objectively measuring employees who report to her.

Something to remember if you are new to the game or lack confidence in your ability to measure employees effectively is this: You are not alone. If women have a tendency toward tenderness, so do many men; although in them it is generally perceived as gentleness and wisdom rather than as feather-headed softness. And, while there is nothing wrong with gentling employees within the context of a sound overall management philosophy, too much tenderness can be counterproductive at times. Performance evaluation is one of them. This is the time to be objective, constructive, and helpful.

APPRAISING YOUR APPRAISAL SKILLS

Use this self-test to determine your ability to focus on job performance. If you are totally honest, it can be very revealing. Some good managers who took the test learned, to their surprise, that they were subconsciously giving pluses for characteristics that had nothing to do with quality or quantity of tasks performed.

DIRECTIONS: Select an employee whom you know well and with whom you have been impressed, favorably or unfavorably. Apply to his/her performance an overall job evaluation of *unsatisfactory, satisfactory, good, very good, outstanding.* Then review each of the following and note those factors which may have played a part in your decision.

_____ 1. Good attitude (often in spite of a tough home situation)
_____ 2. Products, projects, ideas that are sound
_____ 3. Attendance—usually on time, rarely takes sick leave
_____ 4. Innovative resolutions to difficult problems

_____ 5. Achievement of specific objectives, tasks within a pre-scribed time frame

_____ 6. Loyalty, especially to me and my programs

_____ 7. Effective implementation of plans directed toward achievement of organizational goals

_____ 8. Good appearance

_____ 9. Acceptance of criticism, advice

_____ 10. Cooperative, even under the most trying circumstances

_____ 11. Consistently high performance, measured against standards

_____ 12. Productive, responsible use of available resources—fiscal, human, material

_____ 13. Good team player

_____ 14. Neat, orderly work area

_____ 15. Good public relations skills

_____ 16. Pleasant personality

_____ 17. Hard-luck syndrome; needs a boost

Scoring

If you were truly honest with yourself and did not answer according to what you thought the answer *should* be but what it *was:*

- Give yourself 10 points for each of the following factors you noted: 2, 4, 5, 7, 11, 12.

   This is the stuff solid, results-oriented performance is made of.

- Give yourself 2 points for each of the following factors you noted: 3, 6, 9, 10, 13, 15.

   These characteristics and traits are helpful and supportive; they *may* help a unit move ahead, but they may *not.* They are not *directly* related to task accomplishment, at least generally.

- Deduct 4 points for each of the following factors you noted: 1, 8, 14, 16, 17.

   These characteristics and traits may be found in the Boy Scout next door or your German shepherd. Whether or not they are channeled productively depends upon many factors.

Total

   50 to 60 points—Terrific.
   40 to 50 points—Not so terrific, but promising.
   30 to 40 points—You've got some learning to do.
   Below 30 points—Study this chapter carefully. You are in real
         trouble.

Suppose your score was not what you wanted it to be. Suppose that you lack confidence in your ability to measure staff members objectively and accurately. What does one do?

One gets tough. Not so tough that one forgets to be honest, objective, and constructive. But one gets tough in the sense that personalities or divorces or mortgage foreclosures are placed in proper perspective and do not become, along with a pleasant attitude and neat office, reasons not to address poor performance.

Next, one establishes a process. There is a real advantage if an MBO (management by objective)-type system (by whatever name) is in place. If not, there are important steps you can take before attempting further performance evaluation.

The first depends upon prerogatives. Are you free to select a performance appraisal system for your department or even for the total organization? Must you follow a poor system already established and imposed upon you? Regardless, you can take the initiative and insist—even if it is just in your own department—on solid performance *planning* as the critical part of performance evaluation.

We have outlined below our favorite approach. It follows elements of a number of systems and, as a single system, has been tested in both large and small organizations. It works. It provides as much objectivity as reasonably can be infused into an activity that must, by its very nature, have a goodly amount of subjectivity to it. The idea is to increase objectivity and reduce subjectivity.

PERFORMANCE PLANNING

If you are measuring production of widgets, performance planning is a simple matter. In the next 12 months, Joe Smith (1) will increase the number of widget handles he makes by 5 percent over last year; (2) will reduce rejects in his output by 10 percent over last year; and so forth. It is not so simple if Joe administers a grants program which includes a lot of variables, a lot of contact with the public, a lot of oversight of others' work. There are still objective measurements, but they may not be as obvious.

Performance planning begins with laying out the turf, determining who is responsible for what broad area of activity. Within that area, departmental or unit goals and objectives must be established for the measurement period and beyond (see "The Planning Mystique"). Job descriptions must be updated to reflect honestly and completely the tasks to be performed. They should include the signature of both employee and supervisor, indicating that there is understanding about the tasks.

Now that it has been clarified in writing who is doing what, it is necessary to develop performance standards—the criteria against which you will review performance and, ultimately, make decisions about merit increases and promotions. There are many kinds of standards, some more obvious than others, such as in the case of Joe Smith, widget maker. Basically, however, there are some key categories of standards which should be helpful:

- Positive standards, which indicate something you want to happen (increase production by 10 percent)
- Negative standards, which indicate something you do not want to happen (reduce complaints from the public by 50 percent)
- Comparative standards, which measure against another established standard (place more women and minorities in management jobs than the Chicago division does)

- Historical standards, which measure against previously established indices (these can also be positive, negative, or comparative)
- Designed standards, which are written to meet a highly specific outcome and which really cannot be categorized generally (complete negotiations for Policy X by June 1)

Standards should be relevant, achievable, and measurable within some kind of time frame. The point of all of this is to be able to put down in writing a criterion that will tell what conditions will exist when the job is well done.

Exactly what will be the circumstances when the task has been accomplished as promised? The performance standard becomes an agreement—not legal, but formal—between employee and supervisor as to how well a job will be performed.

Things to remember about setting performance standards:

1. Most individuals will set higher standards for themselves than their supervisors would set for them.
2. The employee who commits to a certain level of performance has a stake in the outcome: it is his or her *word,* and keeping that word becomes an important goal.
3. Expect employees to be "up" about meeting and exceeding standards. It is part of the psychology and the motivation.
4. Standards are not easy to write. The employee should have some help in drafting some initial statements. If you cannot provide that help, identify someone who can. Together you can refine and develop them.
5. Almost every task can have a measurable standard, even if it is negative—"no complaints."

Once the standards are established and agreed upon, is that all there is to it until 12 months have passed and it is time for evaluation and merit raises? Hardly. It is important to conduct work progress reviews along the way. Whether they are every two, three, or four months will depend upon the nature of the work and your own planning.

The final evaluation generally coincides with merit-raise time and is used as a basis for determining the level of salary increase. However, this does not need to be the case. Some organizations prefer to focus on the performance evaluation in a different light, such as identification of promotion potential—one separated entirely from salary.

Two final things to remember about the one-on-one progress review or final evaluation: (1) The immediate supervisor does the review, not a manager up the line who knows the employee by little more than name and title. (2) Evaluation is one-on-one in every sense of the term. It requires two people in a quiet room with no observers and plenty of time for honest discussion.

PERFORMANCE APPRAISAL

Carefully review a comprehensive job description with clearly defined responsibilities, using your own or someone else's for practice. Use the following as a guide to work through the process of performance planning, review, and appraisal. In real life you will want to revise the form to allow more space for writing and to make it consistent with the number of performance reviews you wish to make during the performance year.

Part I. Enter employee's name, job title, department, and supervisor.

Part II. Note the dates you plan to have each task completed. When the task is actually done, correct the dates if necessary.

Part III. Using the updated job description, select up to five *key* responsibilities against which you wish to measure performance. (It is not necessary to measure against every responsibility; measuring against key responsibilities or tasks is more productive).

Part IV. For each key responsibility, write at least one performance standard.

Parts V and VI. Part V, in real life, would be completed during review sessions with the employee. At that time, frank discussions would focus on progress to date, problems, quality of supervision. Corrective measures would be planned. Part VI is the final appraisal, where determination is made regarding overall performance.

Part I

Name_____

Job Title/Code_____

Department/Unit _____

Supervisor/Appraiser_____

Part II: Time Schedule

Job description updated, signed by supervisor, employee_____

Initial meeting to discuss performance standards_____

Performance standards written, agreed upon_____

First review scheduled_____Second review_____

Final appraisal scheduled_____

Part III: Key Responsibilities	**Part IV: Performance Standards**
1._____	_____
2._____	_____
3._____	_____
4._____	_____
5._____	_____
Employee signature_____	_____
Supervisor signature_____	

Part V: Performance Review * | Date

1.

2.

3.

4.

5.

* For each responsibility, state where the employee is in relation to meeting the agreed-upon standard as *above, at,* or *below standard.* This is a review, not a final appraisal.

Part VI: Final Appraisal

	1.	2.	3.	4.	5.
Most often exceeded standard					
Most often met standard					
Most often did not meet standard					

Employee comments:

Supervisor comments:

Date

THE OTHER SIDE OF PERFORMANCE APPRAISAL: BEING APPRAISED

Performance evaluation can be the most effective tool for professional and personal development the job situation can offer. Correctly managed, it provides a mechanism for setting reasonable goals, for measuring one's performance against those goals, for identifying strengths and improving weaknesses. Employees who look upon performance review as something akin to having a wisdom tooth pulled are missing a very important boat. Those who use the process to their advantage are the ones on their way up.

To use it to *your* advantage, you must take both the concept and the process of performance evaluation seriously. As you participate in setting performance standards, give the task your best effort. Monitor your own performance against those standards. Make certain you meet all of them; work to exceed some. During performance reviews, make every effort to accept evaluative statements objectively. Enhance your strengths, minimize your weaknesses.

If, in spite of your commitment to objective performance evaluation, the process isn't working well for you, it may be because your manager has fallen into one or more of the typical traps that plague some managers. Unfortunately, these traps are all *too* typical! Some are discussed below, along with tips on what you can do to make things better.

- Managers may be afraid to file a report that looks too good, for whatever reason. These timid leaders will apologize for a mark that is unfairly low, noting that they "had to find something to mark down; otherwise, nobody will believe this is an honest evaluation."

Anytime a manager says she must "grade you down to make the report believable," tell her you'd rather have honesty now and risk the credibility gap later.

- Managers may be fearful about letting you participate in setting performance standards. For whatever reason, they lack confidence in the ability of their staff members to make realistic assessments of their own ability to perform.

Insist that performance standards be mutually agreed upon. Remind your boss that employees normally set higher standards for themselves than their supervisors will set for them. Be courteous. Be insistent. Be firm.

- Scheduled performance review sessions may be postponed or delayed until the measurement criteria are out of date and the work accomplished is ancient history.

MANAGEMENT STRATEGIES FOR WOMEN

Be a squeaky wheel if you must, but try to make the noise as melodious as possible. Insist that performance review sessions be held as near to the scheduled dates as possible. Let your manager know how much you respect her for keeping the dates, when others around her are not so conscientious.

- If there is no real commitment to the system, or if a manager is lazy, she may do a slipshod job of clarifying duties, agreeing on standards, and following through on reviews. If extra paperwork is involved for outstanding performance, she may not indicate that *anything* is outstanding.

Become totally familiar with the evaluation process so that you can tactfully remind the boss of what isn't happening that should be. Let her know how much it means to you to be judged on the basis of your performance, how this kind of evaluation motivates you to work harder than ever, how proud you are to be on her team.

- Even if the system is in place and reasonable objectives established, managers may ignore the facts and score a staff member based on factors totally unrelated to performance.

If you feel that you have been judged against factors unrelated to performance and the score doesn't match up with points earned, ask for an explanation.

- Some managers simply will not discuss performance. They are unable to move this whole area from an emotional to a managerial context. They feel any comment is a negative criticism. They fear they will be misinterpreted. These are the folks who suffer mightily when deciding on merit raises.

If your manager balks at discussing performance and you have tried all the above, discuss the matter with the director of personnel. It may constitute a risk, but is also may result in some much-needed help for the manager. Personnel directors are supposed to be discreet. Let's hope yours is.

- Some managers make promises during a performance evaluation that they will not or cannot keep. If they think things are going well and want to encourage you to even greater performance, they may promise promotion or a substantial raise. If things are not going well, they may promise to provide some training even though there are no training monies available.

Take any off-the-cuff promises in an evaluation session with a grain of salt, unless there is a written follow-up. You can, however, use these spontaneous comments as a clue to what your manager is thinking.

- Fear of being considered prejudiced may keep a manager from evaluating fairly an ethnic minority or female staff member. The manager may inflate an evaluation just to let others know that she is on the right side of the civil rights issue.

Let your boss know that being female or an ethnic minority means being treated equally and fairly—no advantages, no disadvantages. Inflated evaluations usually can be detected. Eventually, they will do more harm than good, however lofty —or cowardly—the intentions.

- Some people truly cannot criticize in a helpful and constructive way. Whatever they offer turns out to be negative and demeaning.

Try to sift out the worthwhile message from the unkind comments. Attempt to understand the manager's inability to offer constructive criticism. If she cannot be positive, show her you can. Respond to a belittling remark with sincerity. It may change things. It may not, but you'll feel better about the situation.

- For performance appraisal to work, managers must be prepared to deal with its reciprocal nature. Some cannot.

Be honest and direct when giving feedback about your manager's supervision as it affects your own performance on the job. If you find that she is unable to accept this kind of information, quit trying to offer it. There are other ways to get the message across, although they may not be as effective and certainly will be more time-consuming. Here's an example:

One of us was appraising the performance of a bright, talented, and competent female supervisor. During the discussion, the supervisor said, "You sometimes tell me to do something in half-sentences and dash off, leaving me confused and uncertain about what you want. Please don't do that anymore!" I didn't. The supervisor took appropriate advantage of the appraisal process to correct a problem rather than trying to seek clarification each time she received confusing instructions.

All the foregoing assumes that the organization or department has an objective evaluation system in place. If it does not, and you find yourself being measured against criteria that have nothing to do with performance, you may want to work for a better system by:

1. Volunteering to serve on an ad hoc personnel or employee relations committee where this kind of system can be promoted.
2. Encouraging the boss to consider implementing a system at department level.
3. Volunteering to do some research for the boss on employee evaluation and motivation.
4. Suggesting that you and your boss experiment with setting performance standards for your position. Then *perform,* work together on reviewing and appraising performance, and expect positive results.

17. Beating the Boardroom Blahs
A Guide to Conducting Effective Small-Group Meetings

A MEETING is like the production of a play: it needs to be planned before the doors are opened to a crowd. In addition, both contain critical elements of success—a director, a script, behind-the-scenes work, a stage, and, finally, the actors and their performance. If one or more of these parts lacks excellence, the way is set for a flop or, at best, a ho-hummer.

THE DIRECTOR

This is a strange role. While the director is the principal force behind a successful production, she must work in such a way that she remains in the background rather than on stage-front

153

when the curtain opens. In the end, the actors may get the applause, but the director will get the credit. It is the same (or should be) for anyone chairing a meeting.

If you have had the opportunity to observe a group of rehearsing actors whose director is absent, you probably noticed that someone eventually took on the role of the missing director, even if that someone was not assigned or expected to do so. We have heard about this aspect of group behavior for years—a leader will emerge when there is a gathering of people for a common purpose. The director, understanding this behavior, will not want to relinquish her responsibility to provide direction for a lengthy period of time. Neither should a chairwoman, or she will soon find someone in the group has stepped forward to assume the leadership role. She must, instead, direct her cast to an end. Finally, a director knows a good show is the result of hard work and meticulous preparation before and during rehearsals.

Similarly, the chair must recognize the links between agenda planning and agenda management. As much energy must be devoted to one as to the other if the meeting production is to be cohesive and worthwhile. Unfortunately, this basic tenet is often overlooked by managers.

The following will provide some "stage-right" details for the chairwoman as director of board meetings, committee get-togethers, or formal staff meetings.

A POWERFUL SCRIPT

The impact of effectively formulating and organizing the material from which a group must work can be summarized in these words about Shakespeare: The Bard was able to "cram together, second for second, a quantity of lively material of incredible richness. This material exists simultaneously on an infinite variety of levels; it plunges deep and reaches high."*

* Peter Brook, *The Empty Space* (New York: Atheneum, 1969).

Meeting agendas should not be much different. If you do not have a good script to start with, your players will be ineffective. They cannot offer more than what is called for by the author.

The first step to a powerful script is good agenda composition. There are two basic points to consider at the outset: (1) if you can put it into a memo, don't put it on the agenda; and (2) have a clear purpose behind every meeting you hold and behind every item on the agenda.

Unless the chairperson understands the results she wants to achieve, she will be unable to design strategies to reach those results or to measure success or failure when it is all over. In addition, a clear purpose assists the participants in understanding what is required of them and promotes quality contributions during the meeting.

NOTE: When you call for the submission of agenda items, be wary of the individual who requests time on the program but cannot tell you just what it is that he wants from the group. He may be one of those who believe that his status is enhanced by the number of times his name appears on the agenda.

Every item should require some kind of action by the group. So, for each topic ask yourself questions like these:

- Do I want discussion only, someone's contribution in particular, approval, veto, recommendation?
- If it is a discussion item requiring no action from the committee and relating to no urgent problem, should I remove it from the agenda?
- Do I want a solution decided *at* the meeting?
- Do I want those present to offer suggestions concerning how to implement something?
- Do I want to divide the group into smaller groups for the purpose of handling a number of responsibilities—perhaps form subcommittees?
- Do I want an analysis from the group?
- Do I want to know how a change in policies or procedures will affect all organizational areas represented at the meeting?
- Do I want the group to brainstorm or systematically analyze problems in a more structured way?

The point of all of this is to think through the contribution you want from the participants once the agenda item is before them. Now that you know, will others know what is expected of them? It helps to include a concise, written goal statement with each agenda item.

As the final steps in script composition, put all topics in priority order. Determine the estimated time it will take to complete each item and start cutting the agenda from the bottom if you have a monster on your hands.

Thespians know that a dull theater experience usually involves repetition—the "deadly" writer or director "uses old formulas, old methods, old jokes, old effects, stock beginnings to scenes and stock ends. . . . A deadly director brings no challenge to the conditioned reflexes that every department [in the theater] must contain."*

Deadly meeting experiences have many of the same qualities. Who says you cannot start a meeting with the hottest topic on the agenda? Who says you cannot eliminate those boring standing committee reports if they require no action or discussion, and contain no updates on important projects? Who says it is not your responsibility to make certain that presenters try to be interesting as well as excellently prepared? Who says all discussion must take place at the boardroom table rather than at the luncheon table? And who says you have to have lunch, coffee breaks, and the reading of the minutes at the same hour each meeting? Meeting goers probably could add a dozen other ideas for breaking out of the same old agenda mold.

There is one organizational idea, however, that *should* be repeated for each meeting. *Organize the agenda in such a way as to make your meeting move along.* Even to the point where silence is action! How about trying these suggestions?

- Start off with a bang of a topic (probably your first priority) when everyone will be fresh, alert, and able to deal with tough issues.
- Try placing another top-priority and exciting idea immediately after a meal break, when everyone needs to wake up.

* Peter Brook, same book.

156

- Avoid piggy-backing heavy agenda items without allowing a break from intense mental activity. Intersperse short, lighter topics that can give the group a respite from pressure.
- Break long topics into shorter segments to facilitate discussion and to generate the feeling of getting a lot accomplished.

BEHIND-THE-SCENES WORK

Unfortunately, all the printed word can tell us is what is planned, not how the agenda actually is going to come alive. Here are some suggestions to help turn planning into reality:

- The agenda should be sent out a week prior to the meeting. Before that, members will lose the materials or postpone required homework until the last minute. If the agenda is mailed later, conscientious individuals will complain about not having enough time to prepare adequately, and they are correct in doing so. Keep in mind the possibility of delays in the mail when you set your mailing date. And don't forget to include *all* supportive documents in the package. Passing out papers at the meeting is often considered an annoyance. Too, people should not be expected to read and make decisions about information in a few short minutes.
- If you are expecting some new faces at the meeting, take time to learn something about the bodies to which they are attached. Avoid surprises from unknown sources. On the other hand, you will want to make certain that new people feel welcome to speak and that they are not intimidated by the committee veterans. Some preliminary familiarizing can solve these potential problems.
- If you feel strongly about a certain agenda item, arrange to have someone else present your initial argument. The action serves several purposes. First, as chairwoman (and probably the boss) you already have more authority than the remaining members. To disagree with the boss is suicide in the minds of some and a visible demonstration of antagonism by others. Second, a chairwoman's job is to orchestrate all the elements of a meeting so objectives are met. It is somewhat like the director who does not also play the leading role so that she can sit back in the audito-

rium and view the play as a whole. Some good chairpersons have made it a rule to say less than what they are thinking. Of course, it is still essential to speak up when you believe you should, as long as there is balance between monopolizing the discussion and contributing to its value.

- Consider telephoning ahead of time those people who have considerable interest in or potentially significant contributions to make to a particular topic. These preliminary conversations can demonstrate your interest in hearing from others, serve as a signal for others to do some premeeting research, and help uncover and defuse potential railroading or sabotaging of plans.

THE STAGE

In the early theater days, players who wanted to be noticed stood near the front of the stage, where illumination was greatest from the limelights. Today's staging is more complicated, with the advent of highly technical lighting equipment. But ask any good actor where the "hot spots" are on a normally illuminated stage and he can lead you directly to them. Research in the theater tells us that some stage locations are more powerful than others. The chairwoman's boardroom table is filled with similar spots. As leader, it is important to know where they are so they can be used as tools for better direction and for prevention of up-staging by your scene-stealing players.

In order to serve as the official guide at the meeting, the chairwoman should sit at the head of the table. It is the best vantage point from which to view all individuals. All focal lines culminate at that spot, which means that it is the place to be to gain attention when you need to do so.

For the leader, the second most important spot to consider at a long table is that directly opposite her. It, too, can serve as an equal power point if someone decides to use it as such. We have known employees who consciously parked their gear opposite the top spot with every intention of taking over the leadership of the meeting. The reasons? Because (1) they used to be chairperson and were unable to relinquish the role gracefully, (2) they wanted to intimidate the chairperson by negative gestures and reactions, or (3) management changes were in progress and they wanted to use the meeting setting as a forum or to call attention to themselves. On the positive side, the chairwoman can use the position to (1) draw attention to a particular employee whom she wants noticed, (2) focus attention on a proponent who will provide moral and verbal support on a difficult issue, or (3) seat individuals while they are making presentations.

The psychology behind the face-to-face positioning also can be transferred to other members seated at the table. If you have several employees who have a penchant for arguing with each other, it may be helpful to avoid seating them opposite each other. Sometimes the face-to-face arrangement gives them a better confrontation opportunity. Check it out yourself. Watch the argument scenes on television some evening and see which way the characters are positioned. The believable scenes will be toe-to-toe confrontations.

The positions of least status are those behind any seat at the conference table. Therefore, a good chairperson will see that all bona fide participants at a meeting are positioned at the table. Visitors and observers can occupy the sidelines. And anytime a person is brought from this "chorus line" or "audience" position, his or her status will be enhanced in the process.

In some boardrooms, all individuals are seated according to rank, with the chairperson or chief executive officer seated front and center, the senior vice president (or next officer in rank) seated to her right, and the second-most-important officer seated to her left. Seniority and rank determine the distance down the table's sides where everyone else is placed. Junior officers may be just within shouting distance of the chairperson, while the Old Guard sits at her elbows.

Interestingly, even when there is no prescribed seating order, people may seem to perceive one, with placement near the power denoting importance. You may find that there are certain staff members who arrive early for each meeting to grab a "top" chair along the side of the table. Heaven help any newcomer who inadvertently takes a chair so "reserved." Other members may make it a habit of arriving late, scrunching down in the chairs at the far end of the table.

Observing who sits where can tell you something about your staff, task force, or committee. Try keeping a record over several meetings for your own edification. Use Boardroom Musical Chairs, which follows.

BOARDROOM MUSICAL CHAIRS, OR WHO IS SITTING WHERE AND WHY?

Noting where people sit when they are part of a staff, board, or committee that meets with some semblance of regularity can provide a fascinating key to certain of their feelings. Who consistently wants to be close to the power? Who wants to keep some distance from the power and why? Keep track of seating placements over several meetings for some important clues. (Use a chart such as the one illustrated to note who sits where.) Then, at later meetings, try moving the power to the opposite end of the table or to the center of the table along one of the sides. Make a note of how the others rearrange themselves.

AGENDA MANAGEMENT

The most important function of the chairwoman at the meeting is to guide participants toward the final goal of each agenda item. Heaven knows, it is not always easy if either the issues or players have the potential of being volatile! Here are some suggestions to help you encourage positive progression toward agenda goals:

1. Make certain all issues or tasks are well defined at the outset so discussion stays on track. Continue to clarify the problem if it becomes muddy. Quickly bring strays back into the fold.
2. For each agenda item, make certain everyone understands what

The
Power!

The Hot
Spot

is expected of the group. (Example: a vote or a recommendation.)

3. Assist the group by interpreting comments when needed or by restating something for emphasis.

4. Ask for information and facts that are pertinent to the agenda item when it becomes apparent that not all information has been made available.

5. After a lengthy discussion, summarize what has been said and pull ideas together if participants have difficulty connecting the pieces.

6. If the group is at a standstill, either provide or ask for suggestions on how to proceed.

7. When a viable solution has been identified or if participants begin repeating themselves, then the agenda item should come to closure. If someone else has not already done so, the leader should offer a decision or conclusion for the group to consider, accept, or reject.

8. If it becomes apparent that there are more questions than answers concerning an issue, or that the topic is too large or complex to finish, or that others not at the meeting should be consulted before further action is taken, halt discussion of the issue. However, *some* action should be taken in addition to terminating discussion. Determine to do further research, form a study group, set a specific time to reconsider the issue, or decide to take *no* action on the problem. (We recall one chairperson who was terrific at staying on her time schedule but was terrible about getting a group to take action at the right time. If the time indicated on the planned agenda elapsed in the midst of a positive and substantive discussion, down went the gavel. Or if a decision had been reached prior to the time indicated to move to the next topic, she continued discussion unnecessarily.)

As important as the techniques to guide the group toward agenda goals are the methods you use to keep the group in good working order.* The following may help:

- Insert humor when appropriate or call for a coffee break if you need to reduce tension. Sound obvious? It is, but when tension

* There are many good references on positive, productive group relationships and communications. A favorite of ours is an "oldie but very goodie" by K. D. Benne and P. Sheats, "Functional Roles of Group Members," *Journal of Social Issues,* Vol. 4, number 2, 1948.

is running highest and we need a break the most, we often get so involved ourselves that we forget the obvious.

- Keep communications channels open by getting others to explore their differences or to compromise when necessary.
- Encourage wide participation. Invite quiet members to enter the discussion. To avoid discussion monopolization, politely show impatience for those who talk too much or suggest a time limit for speakers.
- Be friendly. Show responsiveness through words or body language.
- Encourage participants by recognizing their contributions.

THE ACTORS

As one of the players, rather than the director, can your role be effective? Can it have influence? Can you use it to gain star billing in the future? Yes to all the above. Depending on the *quality* of your participation, you can make your role an important stepping stone toward life at the top.

Here is a baker's dozen helpful hints:

1. Think of yourself not as a member of the audience who is in the theater to sit back and be entertained. Recognize that you are a player with a role to perform.
2. Think about this role; speculate on the influence or impact your performance can have on others. Will they find you helpful and interesting? ("Say, that's a terrific idea, and well stated!") Or will they find you redundant and dull? ("We tried that idea two years ago. And why doesn't she get to the point of what she's trying to say?")
3. Never attend a meeting unprepared.* Do your homework.

* There are two schools of thought on the wisdom of advance preparation. In his excellent book, *Managerial Psychology*, (University of Chicago Press, 4th ed., 1978) Harold J. Leavitt says, "For some, 'preparation' may mean that each man works out his individual position before the meeting and then comes into the group to try to sell his position to the rest." If the selling job fails, Leavitt warns, the individual "may feel he has suffered a personal, egoistic defeat." Other experts warn of advance politicking, of critics developing opposition strategies during the preparation period. Though these risks are real and substantial, we believe they are justified by the benefit of receiving the thorough and thoughtful involvement of others.

This means more than a cursory glance at the agenda; it means researching and inquiring and thinking about the topics to be discussed and/or decided on at the meeting.

4. When you have something to say, say it well. Think about the contributions you want to make ahead of time, and structure them so that you (a) immediately speak to the point; (b) present back-up information in a logical, one, two, three style; (c) conclude with a strong, positive statement; (d) be as brief as possible.

5. When two sides of an issue are being discussed and you are speaking for one, address your remarks principally to those in your own camp; establish frequent eye contact with the undecided, to whom you address some of your strongest points. Build your case through positive strategies. Avoid the negative trap of trying to convince those who are 100 percent on the other side. They aren't listening; they are anxiously waiting for their turn to state their own case.

6. Watch and listen for feedback. While some of those in the room may make verbal responses that are helpful, don't fail to observe the signals others may be sending.

7. As other players perform, analyze what is going on around you. Note the alliances that are made or abandoned. Observe the by-play and politicking. Watch the chairperson and see how she operates. Would you do her job differently? This is great on-the-job training for future stellar roles.

8. Hang on to your emotions, even if those around you do not. If someone offers a tasty morsel, check for hooks before you bite and perhaps lose your composure.

9. Remember some basic rules of etiquette: Don't speak while others are speaking. Don't tell secrets or whisper to those around you. Don't pass notes. Remember what listening means —*applying* oneself to hearing something.

10. Dress appropriately for your role. This is an opportunity for others to see the total you. Along with performance, they will notice costuming.

11. Forget the adage about never volunteering. Volunteer to do tasks you believe you can do well.

12. If you are the lone female cast for the meeting, don't complain to everyone about the situation. Instead, develop some strategies to remove barriers which typically may exist. Here are

three suggestions: *(a)* Always use two very effective communications skills—*supportive listening* and *assertive communication* (see "The Woman's Glossary"); they will markedly reduce problems of misunderstanding. *(b)* Try to have some information that others do not have; use it to gain their attention. *(c)* Offer a new idea or plan which is so unique, good, bad, or controversial that they will have to abandon their "old-boy" huddle to explore it with you. These tactics will help change a habit of ignoring female involvement to one of recognizing and, one hopes, respecting it.

13. Should you agree to take notes? In essence, we hold that you should if the activity will work to *your* benefit, and that you should *not* if the role will present either an emotional or professional problem for you.*

* Note taking can put an individual in a terrific inside position. It *can* work to one's benefit, if the situation is handled well and with Number One uppermost in the decision to take this usually undesirable role.

18. Creative Conferences

conference: *A compulsive phenomenon that strikes homogeneous groups at least once yearly, causing them to flock together, hire very important speakers at outrageous costs, print name tags and other materials, order London broil and fruit cups by the hundreds, tolerate hostile hotel staffs and, finally, wonder* why.

More and more professionals are not only *wondering* why, they are *asking*. Time is precious, and people are careful about wasting it. Schedules are so crowded with managing, meeting, traveling, negotiating, reporting, and surviving, that it is difficult to block out a period of days for *any* purpose. And, when the purpose and the value are not apparent, people are likely to say, "No, thank you. Not this time."

Much that is good can result from a purposive, well-planned

conference that sets out to *do* something. But too often conferences are not worthwhile. The reasons? Most often, because:

1. People are brought together primarily for the sake of tradition.
2. There are no objectives for the conference—no real purpose, no hoped-for results or outcomes.
3. Attention focuses on high-priced guest speakers who deliver great messages but fail to communicate with their audiences.
4. The conference has no enduring quality or lasting impact. Its final report is received, placed on a shelf, and promptly forgotten. Nothing happens. Nothing has changed.

Professional conference planners have their own way of doing things, but most of us who find ourselves with a major conference to plan and direct are not professionals in the field. Instead we are managers in a different discipline, people called upon by our company to get people together for a reason.

What can one do to put a little creativity into the works and, at the same time, ensure that details are handled? A number of things, which can be categorized as planning, conducting, and following up. And, if one has the resources and expertise available, one can take advantage of a new and exciting conference format—teleconferencing. Let's look first at the traditional elements (which are also included in a teleconference) and then look briefly at the mechanics of the electronic meeting.

PLANNING

Define the purpose of the meeting and set reasonable and relevant objectives before you do anything else. Use these as your guideposts as you plan content, schedule, logistics, and promotion.

CONTENT

Begin by making a list of what conferees should hear about, learn about, and share during the meeting. Plan content around the topics on your list. Do not be seduced by others into including discussions, slide shows, side shows, great new films, or anything else that is not germane. Frame your sessions around powerhouse questions or answers—"Is lung cancer preventable?" or "How to know if you are likely to develop lung cancer," rather than "A report on lung cancer among women."

Provide a format mix to hold attention. Use speakers, workshops, films, discussions, role playing. Avoid interminable and dull panel presentations. If you use panels, try the style of newsman Martin Agronsky, where panelists *discuss* and *debate* issues with each other. It is an entertaining and fascinating improvement over the traditional presentation—each speaker performing in sequence, followed by questions from the floor and answers by the panel. One still can have a question-and-answer period. But be prepared; the audience is going to be fired up after such a lively beginning.

Include guest speakers who have something new, significant, meaningful, or unexpected to say about the topic.* Don't be surprised if, in a later evaluation, participants say they would have preferred having had more time to listen to each other than to the guest speakers, no matter how good they were. "We never have enough time to talk to each other, to learn from each other" is a frequent complaint with which we are uncomfortably familiar.

Provide *helpful* back-up material on the topics presented. Do not encumber those attending with a basketful of printed stuff that will end up in another basket. Make certain that every handout is worthwhile. Unclutter the conference.

Try to have one great gimmick—an innovation in your field, a fascinating new discovery, an earth-shaking announcement, an appearance by the first woman to grow tomatoes on Mars. One gimmick. Just one. And only if it, or she, is germane.

Select all speakers and presenters based on their *expertise,* not

---

* Some skilled conference planners ask for an advance outline of each speaker's message to make certain that content is relevant and that two or more speakers do not cover the same information. Asking for an outline in advance must be done tactfully; suggesting any change must be done even more tactfully.

prestige. (This is not contrary to the observation above. We assume you will have the Martian gardener only if she relates directly to the purpose of your conference.) Prestige often disappoints; expertise rarely does.

SCHEDULE

Morning hours are the best for getting and holding the attention of conference goers. Early evening opening sessions are good, as long as they do not extend too long and do not follow a heavy dinner. It is best to schedule sitting-and-listening events during the alert times and activity sessions (workshops, discussions, small-group caucuses) during the times when it is more difficult to hang on to an audience.

Remember that the conference day has three parts: morning, afternoon, and evening. Most likely there will be luncheon meetings, perhaps breakfast meetings, and certainly dinner meetings or banquets. If the full range of schedule opportunities is used, expect to have participants operating on half their cylinders—attending more and enjoying it less. Use two of the three parts of any day for business. Allow one part of the day for individual activity. If the conference continues for several days, try scheduling a free morning on the day after an evening event has kept people up late. If the day's schedule includes a breakfast meeting, a full morning agenda, a luncheon, plus an afternoon session, give the troops an evening off. Most likely they will continue to flock together to share and learn and enjoy, but with a feeling of relaxation.

LOGISTICS

Many a great conference has gone down the unstopped drain. There is nothing more distressing than hotel bathtubs that cannot be stoppered for a hot soak before bed, terrible food, paper-thin walls, rooms that are too hot or too cold, shuttle service that forgets to shuttle. Make certain that every single logistical detail is checked, rechecked, and checked again before the conference. Do not rely on telephones or letters; send an aide to the site to look the facilities over in person, meet with the chef, and talk to the management. Do these things before making a commitment to reserve space.*

Other details to check include adequate lighting and ventilation in meeting rooms, public address equipment, podiums, and the like. Are there secretarial and copying services available? Is there a system in place to receive and deliver messages during the conference? And is there a listing of emergency services should there be a need?

Don't guess and never assume. Know.

What about using a little creativity in selecting a site for your conference? A promising place to start is with universities that have their own conference centers. Some are bright and new and modern, others old and wonderfully charming.† Anyone can do the big hotel scene. Try to avoid it in favor of something unique and interesting. It is important, however, to select a center that can be reached conveniently by public transportation and that has the creature comforts you need. Beyond these basic considerations, experiment a little. Sometimes scheduling a winter conference at a summer resort, or vice versa, can result in low-cost conferencing, fabulous facilities, attentive service, and unusual concern. Avoid the crowds. And don't mix priorities. If you get to worrying about whether or not there are enough

---

* Some people only feel comfortable when they do the initial conference site checking themselves. Others admit to not having enough time personally to make a reconnaissance run; instead, they send their most reliable staff assistant on this important mission.

† Two favorites of ours—one of each variety: Endicott House at MIT, Dedham, Massachusetts, is a magnificent old mansion with fireplaces in the bedrooms, the best food this side of the Atlantic, and a staff that treats guests as if they were favorite relatives. Kellogg West, at California Polytechnic Institute, Pomona, California, is modern, convenient, logistically excellent, with very good food and an accommodating staff. We have also enjoyed conferencing in an abandoned mine complex in Death Valley, where guests did their own cooking on kerosene stoves and slept in sleeping bags. And the purpose, learning first-hand about the desert, was well served.

lighted tennis courts or whether the fish will be biting, you have a problem. So will your participants.

PROMOTION

Detailed information about the conference should be sent to potential participants well in advance of the meeting. The reasons for doing so are more complex than assuring that people will be able to schedule the time away and secure flight reservations. You want participants to be thinking about and planning for the event. You want the conference subject to move into minds, take up residence, and occupy space there for a period of time. Forget those who say that announcements too early are forgotten. If the announcements are creative and informative, they will not be forgotten.

Most often several announcements are sent to each conferee, each more specific that the last. The first announcement may be only of the purpose, location, and date of the conference; the next, an overview of topics to be covered and general logistical information; next, reservation forms and preliminary agenda; finally, a wrap-up with detailed information about shuttle services, telephone numbers, and other information conferees will want to include on their own itineraries, as well as the final agenda and a recap of all information previously sent. If fiscal constraints preclude sending several announcements, make one slick package do the job.

It is important to let each person receiving the promotional materials know immediately what is in it for him, if he attends. Frame your promotional package around the answer. Give people a reason to participate.

To what extent the general public is informed about the meeting depends upon your group and the purpose of the meeting. A conference of Lens Polishers of the Greater Telescope Society probably will not want or receive much press. A conference pushing for ratification of the Equal Rights Amendment will want as much press as possible. If you deal with the media, do so honestly and directly. Provide helpful background material and be ready to answer questions. Find out about press deadlines and schedule releases so that no one has an advantage.

Coordinate all public information activities through one individual. Have that individual clear every statement that is released and schedule every interview. It will help you get the kind of coverage and support you want. And for pity sakes, be creative about your press releases, particularly your opening statements.

Typical:

> The Lens Polishers of the Greater Telescope Society will hold their annual conference at Mount Wilson, June 3 to 5. Over 500 lens polishers are expected to attend this 175th meeting of the group.

Creative:

> "I have seen Mars more clearly than anyone in the world," telescope expert John Smith of Des Moines, Iowa, said, Tuesday. "I am convinced it does not have life as we know it, but I am also convinced that it has life forms we need to learn more about."
>
> Smith is one of several scientists who will be present at Mount Wilson, June 3 to 5, to address the 175th annual conference of the Lens Polishers of the Greater Telescope Society.

CONDUCTING

All the planning in the world, all the careful attention to detail can be for naught if the conference itself is not conducted skillfully. The key is a single person in control who can keep everything on schedule, keep nearly everyone at least moderately satisfied, and keep away from hidden agendas. Does this mean that you, as a manager who is skilled at your own job, dare not try managing a conference? No, it does not. It means calling on all your personnel, organizational, negotiation, and communi-

cations skills. It means being prepared for su[
able to handle them. If you have any doubt ab
be the person in charge, don't be. Pick someo1
know is terrific at the job, to be that person. Y(
several individuals to introduce activities and
on-stage duties. But you will use a *single* anchor person—a ια∪∪
that may not be all that apparent to the people out front.

In addition to the person in charge, you will want a *single*
behind-the-scenes coordinator/logistician/unit manager report-
ing to you. Each of your two key individuals may have a staff of
aides, but these people are *their* responsibility.

Use your plans as the score for the performance. Bring to life
their creativity, originality, and relevance. And use them as a
contextual framework for preparing the conference report.

TIPS FOR CONFEREES

Needless to say there is more to a conference than just plans
and a planner. It takes the active and creative participation of
the conferees, as well, to ensure that the conference will be a
success. Following are some suggestions for helping *participants*
get the most out of the experience.

1. Don't go unless you have a good *reason* to go. Define *your*
   purpose and identify what you want to gain from the confer-
   ence.
2. Once you have decided to go, do your homework. Read and
   study any advance information provided. Do some additional
   research if you think it will help *you.*
3. Once on the scene, participate fully. Soak up everything worth
   soaking up. Become involved. Don't be one of those partici-
   pants who makes an appearance at the opening cocktail party
   and at the closing plenary session, with nothing in between. (If
   the conference planners have scheduled you from breakfast
   through midnight, skip out now and then for reasonable rest-
   ing and recouping.)
4. Take notes. Organize them so that they make sense later on,

173

when your motivational factor is not as high. Understand that you may be receiving some information that has not yet been published or shared with others.

5. Make contacts. Exchange business cards. Remember, this is a homogeneous flock. There is much to be learned from others present.

6. Volunteer for continuing activities that are meaningful to you or that may enhance your own career.

7. Remember that any commitments made must be kept. Don't promise to get in touch, critique writings, appear in New York on January 3, unless you will do so.

8. Leave at least one good idea, contribution, or document that will leave your mark on the conference.

9. If you are asked to evaluate the conference, do so honestly and constructively.

10. Review the conference report with care. Key valuable information so that you can make use of it later. Do any follow-up that you want to do *immediately* after the conference. Good intentions fade after the afterglow.

FOLLOWING UP

Something important should happen after the conference is over. It should have done something for everyone present. Motivation and momentum should create a receptivity for follow-up information to sink in, organize itself, and become useful and worthwhile. Something should change as a result of the conference—habits, opportunities, tradition, values, visions, contacts . . . any of a world of possibilities. If everything remains the same, then there was no reason to have the conference.

As the conference giver, you can put this important phase of involvement into motion. You can provide a mechanism through which information and contacts will continue to flow. You can encourage people to continue talking to each other about relevant issues. There may be a reason you will want to form an ongoing task force or inquiry group around a specific hot issue. If there is no reason to have this kind of follow-up, don't create one. People are busy enough. Instead, concentrate on providing a comprehensive, usable, and informative conference report.

Conferees are often asked to complete evaluation statements indicating what parts of the conference were most helpful and what parts were not. Sometimes questions regarding logistics are included. Ask for evaluations *only* if you intend to use the information you collect.

What should be included in the conference report? Normally:

- A summary of conference activities
- A listing of all formal actions taken by conferees
- Abstracts of reports to the conference
- If evaluations were requested from participants, a summary of the data collected
- A roster of participants, speakers, organizers, resource people
- Key information relevant to the conference, its purpose, or its membership; for example, minutes which must be reported, financial summaries, recommendations, forecasts, plans for the future

Include all that is necessary to make your report complete and accurate; exclude extraneous stuff. If you have difficulty telling the difference, ask for advice from associates whose judgement you trust. Sometimes a little distance—your own—is required in completing the conference report. If you have been deeply involved in each step along the way, *everything* seems relevant and worth including. It isn't.

TELECONFERENCING

Teleconferencing allows people across the country to come together in groups to share a common agenda in pursuit of common objectives. Speakers, panel presentations, filmed inserts, live action, and a world of other good things emanating from the origination site are received at several locations around the country. People at the "receive" sites may ask questions and receive answers "on air." They may participate in ancillary activities designed specifically for their receive site. The events are transmitted from one site to several others via a closed-circuit mode. This means that a group gathered at the university center can participate in the program, but your Aunt Mildred, at home, will not get the event on her home television set.

Teleconferencing can be an effective means of communicating important information to a large number of people at diverse locations. Research indicates that consideration must be given to a number of success factors, including preconference planning, ensuring communication and feedback, advance establishment of guides and procedures, and early preparation of conference agenda and ancillary conference materials.*

What about costs, as compared with a traditional format? Program costs (including honoraria, equipment, printed material) may be essentially the same. Logistical costs (including travel, lodging, meals, telephone, shipping of materials) should be significantly less. Service costs (including reporting, recording, clerical, and other assistance) can be at least as much if not more than the traditional mode. Major cost differences are in per capita costs, because hundreds may participate for the cost of tens; and in production costs, where expenses are incurred for the electronic component.

Additional teleconference costs may include the expense of setting up a studio at the conference site or payment for use of an existing studio; the cost of ground lines from the site to a satellite "uplink" or other transmitter; transmission costs to send the program to the receive sites; telephone lines for audio feedback to the origination site so that participants can ask questions and make comments "on air," or additional television capability if there is to be both audio and video feedback; studio costs at the receive site; and fees to the entities that do the electronic planning and production.†

* "After Teleconferencing: A Status Report," *Journal of Communication,* vol. 28, no. 3, Summer 1978.

† This includes the staff costs for broadcast professionals—a producer, director, unit manager, floor manager, camera persons, lighting, sound, and other technicians.

Here is an actual comparison that may be helpful. Approximately 600 women participated in an intensive two-day teleconference at nearly a dozen sites around the country. Per capita cost was approximately $100. This included luncheon both days and all ancillary materials and services at the origination site and the receive sites. A similar conference, covering essentially the same content and with the same goals and objectives, served approximately 50 people at a per capita cost of nearly $800 without the teleconference component. It could not offer the roster of luminaries made possible by the electronic medium. This is not to say the conference was not highly successful or satisfying, for it was both.

Was the teleconference, which reached so many more people at substantially lower cost, also a success? Its conferees reported it overwhelmingly so.* They gave the conference high marks for its overall effectiveness, method of sharing information, and ability to meet its goals.

Another consideration in adding an electronic component is the need for detailed planning. Remember, this is a *program* which will be coming over a television screen. It needs elements that all television programs have if it is to be successful. Read the following excerpts from a planning *agenda* and planning *format*. The format will be prepared from your planning agenda by the production staff.

Agenda

9 a.m. Conference opens
Welcoming remarks by Dr. James Loper
Comments on the satellite experience by David Crippens

9:20 Knowing the Marketplace

Panelists: Deanne Barkley
Diana Dreiman
Maggie Field

* "The Women Writers Satellite Conference: Evaluation and Final Report," by Martha Carrell, Tima Farmy, Diane Tracy; KCET Los Angeles, Calif., April 1979.

MANAGEMENT STRATEGIES FOR WOMEN

Selma Halprin
Harfield Weedin

Questions and answers

Format

Thursday, November 16, 1979: 9 a.m. to 1 p.m., Pacific Standard Time/12 p.m. to 4 p.m., Eastern Standard Time. (Note: two cameras will be used.)

9:00–9:01—Pretaped opening, e.g., typewriter typing credits and information about the Women Writers Teleconference.

9:01–9:04—Pretaped candid comments about writing: a slide/audio montage.

9:04–9:05—Dissolve to wide shot of studio audience with voice-over introducing host.

9:05–9:08—Host with welcoming remarks introduces executive . . .

Is teleconferencing right for *your* gathering? It may be, if your conference involves a substantial number of people, if there is something to be gained by having both a regional or local nature plus a national flavor, if the electronic medium can provide elements that the traditional format cannot, and if you want a conference that is exciting, vital, and unique.

Another plus—conference presentations can be videotaped at relatively low cost during the actual program. The presentations thus become a permanent record and a series of programs for later use.

If teleconferencing seems a viable alternative for you, how do you begin planning for the event? We would recommend, first of all, a call to the Public Service Satellite Consortium (PSSC) in Washington, D.C. The consortium can provide a full package of planning services as well as purchase of transponder time and can have someone from PSSC at your side during the actual conference. Or, if you wish, PSSC can provide a day or two of planning consultation. They are experts in all aspects of teleconferencing.

178

Other organizations can be of help, particularly on a regional level. An example is the Appalachian Community Services Network, a division of the Appalachian Regional Commission, Washington, D.C. The network has designed teleconferences for organizations within its geographical area. Some of the nation's television cable companies (check your Yellow Pages) also can plan teleconferences. Here again, PSSC can help you identify the alternatives open to you.

19. Is Your Computer Embarrassing You?

"I FIND the fear is not so much anymore about these managers having their jobs taken over, although some of that may exist. The fear is more a matter of embarrassment . . . that somehow, there is something they feel they should know about but don't.

"One fellow, an example of many, was asked why he was here. He replied that he wanted to know what his employees are doing. . . ."

Dr. Stuart Madnick, who tames computers every day, knows all about the multitude of problems brought on by the computer age.* He observes that this has been "a concern of some very major companies throughout the United States. It used to be

* Madnick is a computer consultant and associate professor at the Massachusetts Institute of Technology. His doctorate is in computer science.

that computers were quite expensive and limited in performance; therefore, not a lot of businesses had them. . . . As a result, a number of managers have not had an opportunity to be exposed to or have contact with computers."

Now, of course, a great many organizations have computers. And yet, many managers remain unfamiliar with and distant from their electronic neighbors down the hall. The incredible advance of computer technology only adds to the distance. Madnick shared a fascinating analogy: "If the automotive industry had kept pace with the computer industry in terms of technology over the last 25 years, then you could buy a Rolls-Royce for $2.50 and get 12,000,000 miles to the gallon."

Unfortunately, there are managers and boards of directors and presidents of organizations enchanted with the idea of a computer system, with a vision of what they want it to do, but no idea of how to realize the vision. Even discussing their ideas is difficult; the computer world, like so many others, has its own language. And, when they finally overcome this initial barrier, there are others. They have no idea about what's going on in the new computer shop, about how to evaluate its work or make decisions for its future.

Madnick described an executive who had just completed a course in computer technology at MIT as "one of the best managers in the business," who had been put in charge of several thousand employees in the computer area. According to Madnick, the manager did not have the slightest idea of what his people were doing and was determined to find out. "It was intimidating," he said, "because how do you monitor or evaluate employees working for you if you don't have a good concept of what they do?"

For those who wish to avoid being embarrassed by the black box and who want to have a better understanding of the use, misuse, and potential of computers, here is a brief—but hopefully helpful—overview developed from our interview with Dr. Madnick.

THE KEY TO THE BLACK BOX

Q. *How can a manager avoid being intimidated by machines and people in the computer field?*

A. First, realize one should *not* be intimidated. As Dr. Madnick insists, "There is nothing there that is black magic. Computers only can do what they are told to do." Second, acquire an understanding of the concepts of computer operation. This will give you a framework for asking questions of the computer staff, users of the data, and vendors selling equipment. Third, don't be hesitant about asking for explanations. If you aren't getting the message, it is likely that the computer person is not presenting it to you in the right way. Remember, computer folk are an esoteric lot. Madnick advocates, "Make them stop. Back up; try it again, but this time more slowly and precisely."

At first, computer staff who have had little supervision in the past may misinterpret the reason for your questions. They may wonder if you think they aren't performing well. Or they may become impatient. But this will pass when they realize that their manager is sincere about understanding what is going on.

Q. *What is a computer and how does it work?*

A. To answer this question, we went to the Sloan School of Management at the Massachusetts Institute of Technology, one of the nation's leading institutions in computer science.* There we were introduced to the method the school uses to explain what a computer is and how one physically should relate to it. It works like this: There are three basic components of a computer (see the diagram):

* MIT houses the Center for Information Systems Research, partly funded by IBM, Chase Manhattan Bank, General Motors, and other major businesses. MIT faculty also work on a number of innovative projects, such as computerizing the United States Jupiter Mission.

1. *Memory.* This is the place where information is stored for later use. It can be visualized as a rack of numbered mailboxes such as those found in a post office. The more mailboxes you have, the more programs (a well-defined procedure for solving a problem) and data (numeric and nonnumeric information) you can store.

2. *Processor.* This is the device that is capable of performing certain operations as directed by an operator. Basically, this is where the mathematical operations, such as adding and subtracting, take place. It also has a controlling mechanism with two properties: *(a)* it can perform a sequence of steps on its own (called a program) once it has been told the sequence by someone, and *(b)* it can skip steps or change the direction of the steps depending on results of a computation in order to give you a decision. (This is a lot like an IRS form: "If withholding is less than tax, then enter tax minus withholding in You Owe Us box; otherwise, enter withholding minus tax in We Owe You box.")

3. *Input/Output.* This is the method you use to put something in and get it out of the computer. This can be likened to an in basket where people from the outside world have left messages for a make-believe person inside the computer. This little person is allowed to read each slip of paper, do whatever it tells him to do, and print an answer which is then put in an out basket for a real person to collect.

These are the basic concepts. There is one other feature which must be noted—the speed at which the machine operates. It can go through the equivalent of hundreds of hours of manual performance and thousands of procedures in incredibly short time. Certainly the speed of operation is a key factor in the phenomenal growth of computer use in American business.

Q. *What should a manager understand about computers?*
A. 1. Understand the basic computer *hardware.* (Anything you can kick which will hurt you is hardware.) The physical equipment includes *processors* and *memory* (which you now

183

Computer Architecture and Programming

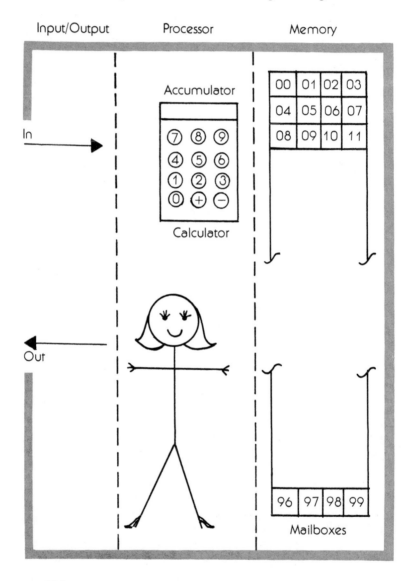

Input/Output   Processor   Memory

Accumulator

Calculator

In

Out

Mailboxes

know about), and *terminals* (a device in a system in which data can either enter or leave.)

2. Understand a few of the basic buzzwords so you have a basis for communication with people working with computers. A good place to begin is to jot down a list of words or phrases of computer jargon that are bandied about your organization. Ask the computer department for definitions, or go to the library for help in decoding your list. The idea is to work with the terminology as it is used in your own realm rather than to work with the entire computer language.

3. Understand the basic concepts of how a computer works. (By now, you do.)

4. Understand *software*. (You don't get hurt if you kick it.) Basically, it includes a set of instructions, which may be extensive or very brief, depending upon the problem. You have to tell the computer what to do with every piece of data you put into it. The total set of instructions make up the program, the well-defined procedure for solving the problem. Here's an analogy: Instructions are the list of ingredients and directions for using them in proper order to make a cake; the whole constitutes a recipe (or program) that can be reused.

5. Get an idea of how hardware and software are related in a computer system. As Madnick explains, it is like a truck (hardware) with a driver (software). The vehicle won't drive by itself, so you need both to make it work. In addition, "the major activity [in setting up a system] is not how much the physical or electronic equipment costs. For most systems today, that's less than one-third the cost. The other two-thirds is in designing what you want it to do and in designing what instructions you want it to follow."*

* Dr. Madnick gave an example of what can happen when a manager does not understand the time and costs involved in the various phases of setting up and running computer systems. A large American firm decided it wanted a new system to computerize a substantial part of its daily activities. A budget was developed, approved by the board, and equipment purchased. The company has since scratched the project because of unanticipated costs. The chief execu-

6. Have a feeling for what a computer is capable of doing today, of not doing today, and of doing in the future.

If you understand the state of the art, you lessen your chances of making a costly financial error when buying equipment. More than one major company has found itself in trouble after it took the vendor's word that the machine could do all sorts of great and wondrous things, only to find that it could not. A few telephone calls to other sources could have enlightened these purchasers. As Madnick says, "If a leading-edge company can do it . . . at least it's feasible. If no one else has done it before, then realize you are a pathfinder and be willing to put up the cash and put up with the ordeal until the bugs are found and exterminated."

Some of the most serious problems in the computer field are mis-expectations. There are two extremes. One is that a manager may believe everything is pure Star Trek: "Computer, do it for me!" The obverse is the manager who misses opportunities to revolutionize his business because his expectations for the computer do not measure up to its capabilities. "I think having a perspective of what things are feasible today would greatly alleviate these mis-expectation problems," Madnick observes.

7. Managers should try to build confidence in their own knowledge of the basics, at least to the point where they feel comfortable enough to ask, "What approach is being taken? What is the timetable? What will programming cost? Who else has done it this way? What is the objective of this system? Who says they need this information?"

Q. *What should a manager not worry about?*

A. According to Madnick, there is nothing a manager might *not* have to worry about. "One of the theories many people operate under is the assumption that 'if I hire good people, then I shouldn't have to worry.' There is some truth to that, but the problem is the definition of *good people* and how to

---

tive had no knowledge of the amount of time, effort, and people it would take to write the programs for the computer and failed to include these costs in his planning budget.

hire them. The field is growing as fast as the technology. Sometimes the computer manager knows only as much as a president on a venture if it's the organization's first time through." He added that it is "becoming much more common for the chief executive *not* to delegate all the computer responsibilities to others. He is keeping better track of what's going on and where the program is going in the computer area." A final note to this answer: We believe that most good managers generally concentrate on the end results and the purpose of their particular computer systems. If the objectives are clearly defined and being reached, there usually is no need for daily tracking of the system. If they are not, then more frequent and intensive contact is required until the system is humming along on key.

Q. *How do you hire good computer people?*
A. "One option for companies is not to do anything too advanced so that they can be certain the people they've hired have done it (a particular project) once, even four or five years ago. Whether deliberately or accidentally," says Madnick, "a lot of larger companies are following this mode of operation.

"The advantage of waiting is that eventually some task will have been done by so many people so many times over that a manager can afford an experienced person for a relatively reasonable price. The trade-off is that his company may be dragging 3 to 10 years behind the leading edge, but he will relieve himself of many management problems. Basically, a company could be in a better management situation if it chose not to be too aggressive and chose instead to follow a few years behind." An added advantage also would be that a manager would "be able to have his own people learn from other people's experience."

The second option could be more costly. If some high-technology company is more concerned with being aggressive and pathfinding in the computer field, then it must hire exceptionally competent and talented people who are able to develop a high state of the art. However, Madnick cautions that the manager of such a company may have to be deeply involved in the development of the system until she is satisfied that it is going well.

Q. *How does a manager know if she should or should not oversee the computer area?*

A. Madnick says you "start by paying attention to it in the first place, and stop once you feel it is under control." We also believe that a manager probably worries less if she knows the people in the organization, is familiar with the end products and objectives of the system, and hears little bickering between users and technicians. But if the boss or the system is new to everyone, she should be as concerned as if she were starting a new business. "A lot of managers," says our favorite computer expert, "become involved when users say, 'Computer people aren't giving me what I need,' or computer types say, 'But they are asking me for something that's impossible to get!' " Madnick suggests that the solution is to get everybody talking—sooner or later somebody has to change. It will be the manager's responsibility to decide who that somebody is.

Q. *What can a manager do to settle disputes between those who deliver computer services and those who receive them?*

A. Consider several strategies, advises Madnick.

1. Have users rate, on a scale of 1 to 10, the usefulness of reports they receive.

2. Have users indicate how much education they have had and want concerning computers. (There is a trend for users to want to know and to control more, especially in organizations where efficiency and effectiveness are measured and reported by computers.)

3. Have both users and technicians rate the education or training their company provides them. (Crucial gaps can be identified and corrective measures taken to improve the competency of both groups. Perhaps these actions also will

increase the ability of each group to communicate more effectively.)

4. Look at the need for restructuring the computer unit. One option is to decentralize the operation, which allows users more direct contact with the system and participation in setting its priorities. (The need for separate staffs and hardware could be a drawback.) The second option is to centralize the unit and establish a planning team of both managers and users who participate in setting directions and priorities. (The principal problem here is the manager who must wait for some time before her much-needed project gets to the top of the priority list.)

5. We would also add to this list the suggestion that managers take a complete inventory of projects and reports that come from the computer shop over the course of a year. The inventory should indicate the frequency of reports and the requesting departments. It may be surprising to learn how much junk can be eliminated to ease computer overload, free computer staff time, reduce unnecessary reports, and separate priority items from information that is "nice to know."

COMPUTER MISUSES/ABUSES TO WATCH FOR

1. Any employee can get access to any information about any person in the computer, if she knows which commands and codes to punch.
2. Security policies are decided by default and happenstance, rather than by high-level management action.
3. Managers treat information about people as if it were a simple asset of the corporation—property that can be used in any way.*

* According to information from an interview with Jeff Meldman, Harvard Law graduate with a computer doctorate from MIT and expert in invasion of privacy via computer, a manager needs to be aware of some important trends in laws governing privacy: (1) "The laws are changing toward a concept of co-ownership of information between business and the data subject. It's as if the

4. A program becomes so large that no one person can understand or correct all of it. For example, many human beings at so many different times, for so many different reasons, can make changes in a program. Unfortunately, a manager cannot often afford to get the mess corrected, because human beings could not possibly handle the computer's volume of work while it is "down."

5. An organization has fantastic equipment and a miserable environment to put it in. A leaky roof, improper air conditioning, poor humidity control, or a host of other nuisances can cause havoc and bring on "down time." Not everything can be blamed on the metal wizard.

6. Unauthorized activities can take place, such as embezzlement, theft, fraud, larceny, vandalism, malicious mischief, extortion, sabotage, espionage. Stanford Research Institute (SRI) has done extensive studies on reported cases of computer abuse. In his book *Crime by Computer,* author Donn Parker uses this SRI data and gives the reader a unique profile of a theoretically vulnerable electronic data processing (EDP) operation:

> The most vulnerable EDP operation performs financial processing and produces negotiable instruments. Employee and management relations are poor, with a high degree of employee disgruntlement. There is a significant lack of separation of tasks requiring a great amount of trust and responsibility. In other words, employees are given wide-ranging responsibilities with minimal checking or observation of their activities. Employees are unsupervised when they are working in the EDP facilities outside normal hours. This weakness is supported by a number of cases that occurred at night or on weekends when employees, especially programmers, were given access to computers for program development work. The computer application programs lack controls to detect anomalous activities and events. The

---

data subject owns part of the file about him or can at least control certain aspects of its correctness, distribution, or its use in decision making. (2) It is becoming the data subject's right to have his/her data kept securely by whoever keeps it. If individuals wish to see what is collected about them, managers will need to be able to gather it all together for *them,* but not others."

programs are difficult to test and provide few opportunities for the development of audit trails, the means by which transactions can be traced from the end product back to the source data. Finally, there is little or no accounting of use of the computer system. Programmers, computer operators, or any employees can use computer services without any direct accountability.*

WHERE CAN I LEARN MORE ABOUT COMPUTERS?

1. Here are some books and journals that we have used and liked ourselves:

- *The Information Age,* by William S. Davis and Allison McCormack (1979, by Addison-Wesley). Extremely basic book on computer concepts for the nontechnical person. Good section on how a computer works, has diagrams and pictures of hardware, and basic glossary.
- *Crime by Computer,* by Donn B. Parker (1976, by Charles Scribner's Sons). Describes new kinds of fraud, theft, larceny, and embezzlement through use of computers.
- *Computers and Management for Business,* by Douglas A. Colbert (1974, by Mason and Lipscomb). Brief but excellent section on what management's involvement should be in the computer area.
- *The Computer Survival Handbook,* by Susan Wooldridge and Keith London (1973, by Gambit). A guide for managers, not technicians. Excellent chapter on lists of questions to ask that help you know if your data processing people are providing you with the best possible service.
- *Computerworld,* a weekly newspaper published by CW Communications Inc., 797 Washington Street, Newton, Mass. 02160. This may help you get insight into the "state of the art" and on new products in the computer field.

2. Sign up for your company program (if one exists) or take a vendor's introductory training program offered for people like

* Donn B. Parker, *Crime by Computer* (New York: Charles Scribner's Sons, 1976).

you (beware of the sales pitch). Also, check with colleges in your area that offer introductory courses for managers.

3. Ask a business friend to let you spend some time with her computer people or to introduce you to the local company that provides services for her organization.

4. Block out some time to spend with your own computer people. (They either will be impressed with your desire to learn or astounded at your stupidity.)

5. Invite computer consultants to make presentations on their capabilities to meet the computer-service needs you have identified for your organization.

6. Invite a "computer type" you respect to lunch twice a week for a month. Trade him/her a bowl of soup for some good advice and knowledge. Then do the same with some users.

20. Task Force Tactics

task force: *1. a specially trained, self-contained unit assigned a specific mission or task, as the raiding of enemy installations; 2. any group assigned to a specific project.*

Webster's New World Dictionary of the English Language

EVERYONE USES task forces these days, but many use them poorly, which is a shame, because they can be an extremely effective management tool. Governors use them to address critical issues in their states, such as energy conservation or air pollution. Corporations use them to measure reaction to future plans. Governmental agencies and public service organizations use them to guide policy development and to measure effectiveness of pet programs. The concept is a good one if properly developed and used. If not, a carelessly conceived task force may end up identifying its creator as the enemy.

What follows are some practical and proven tips concerning forming a task force, establishing controls, planning work activities, budgeting, selecting members, and, finally, killing the beast.

193

FORMING A TASK FORCE

Create a task force—

1. If a task needs to be done and it is not in anyone's job description.
2. When the task crosses departmental lines and needs involvement of people from more than one area or agency.
3. If the task is of *major* importance to your organization and you want to lend it greater visibility.
4. When you don't want a major idea railroaded by a single unit.
5. When you need to build a broad support base.
6. When the issue involved is of particular interest to the public as a whole or a specific public interest group.
7. When it is important to explore an issue, examine alternatives, and formulate recommendations within a rigid time frame.
8. When it is politically smart.
9. If you had a sudden inspiration to form one, quickly took two aspirin, went to bed and slept on the idea, and still feel it is the correct move.

ESTABLISHING CONTROLS

How many times have you seen a task force that never gets the job done, continually asks for more money, schedules extra meetings, debates its purpose, changes its direction, and votes itself immortality? To avoid these pitfalls, establish controls from the very beginning that will guide the task force and its activities from birth to death. You are not guiding its *thinking* or *recommendations;* you are guiding its *activities* and *processes.*

PLANNING WORK ACTIVITIES

- Think through the results you want from the group. If you can't put it in one sentence, then perhaps you have too much for them to do and should seriously think of hiring a staff person for the job. (By all means, avoid bringing a task force on board as a substitute for obtaining staff you need but can't get approved. A task force will never put in 100 percent of its time and effort toward quality work as would someone whose salary increase depends on it.)

- Clearly outline the work to be performed if you want to keep the project from floundering, going out of bounds, or never ending.
- Decide on appropriate activities for task force members. Do you want them to research anything? Pilot-test or validate their products? Produce a report? Conduct a feasibility study? Be responsible for making their results/activities known to any special group(s)?
- Put time lines on each activity, if you want the project to end.
- Another thought to keep in mind: The final result is not a report. In the end, what is the report supposed to help *you* do?
- Finally, we recommend that you give no authority to the task force that you should keep yourself. Have the group make recommendations; you make decisions. Task forces are meant to be an extension of you, not a replacement.

BUDGETING

- Determine how much money you have to spend for task force activities. Once decided, keep to your budget. Negotiate other costs if needed.
- Leave it up to the group to make the best use of the money, but make it clear that there is no tooth fairy waiting in the wings if they contemplate overspending.
- Assign a budget person to be responsible for handling fiscal details.
- Remember, in some cases, the amount of money will determine the scope of the work you can expect from the group.

SELECTING MEMBERS, LIMITING THEIR AUTHORITY

- Always appoint the chairperson yourself. Make certain you select someone who is competent to do the job, is fair and reasonable.

MANAGEMENT STRATEGIES FOR WOMEN

- Select the minimum number of people it takes to do the job. Do not be pressured into adding more people because of political demands.
- Whether you use individuals representing an organization or their own area of expertise depends on what you're after.
- Avoid appointing people who do not work well with others or most of the group's time will be spent arguing and voting.
- Appoint all members yourself so that you can get the quality and mix of individuals you want. As a woman, make certain that both men and women will be represented on your task force and that they will not all be of the same color. Don't cheat yourself out of the marvelous variety of viewpoints you have available to you.
- Do not accept alternates! You shouldn't have a task force unless it is addressing a major problem or issue. Therefore, insist on participation by only those top-rate people you have selected.
- If it is important to the success of your project, you may need to have representation from various geographical locations.

KILLING THE BEAST

- Mark the death date in concrete.
- Periodically remind the members of this date.
- Do not extend the date for completion. If you feel you must, reconstruct the group instead. This will force you to evaluate your own thinking.

TAKING ACTION

The following format, when appropriately expanded and modified for real life, can prove helpful in the thinking stages and organizational process. It is a tactical task force tool.

I. Name of task force _____

II. Reason for formation (background and final use of results)

_____

_____

III. Budget

Travel $_____

Task Force Tactics

Supplies $_____
Consultants $_____
TOTAL $_____

IV. Task force termination date_____

V. Tasks to be completed

	Date Due	Check with project contact before going to next step	
1. _____	_____	____Yes	____No
2. _____	_____	____Yes	____No

VI. Members

Name	Representing	Address	Phone
1.*_____			
2. _____			
3. _____			

VII. Task force reports to _____

VIII. Secretarial help will be provided by

Name_____

Address _____

Telephone _____

IX. Fiscal help will be provided by

Name_____

Address _____

Telephone _____

* Chairperson

197

21. Building a Bandwagon
Women and Ideas

I know they say, "Take it from gut feelings, from first impressions." But I truly believe that most sound ideas have to come from careful thought!

Margaret Adams—National Affairs
Editor, *Good Housekeeping*

Figure out what is important and separate it from what is urgent. The more complex the area you're addressing, the more complex the social organization, the more complex the responsibility, the greater is the pressure to do things immediately. *The most important thing you do today, the best idea, may be laying the groundwork for what you will be doing three years from now.*

Mary King—Deputy Director, ACTION;
cofounder, National Association of
Women Business Owners

Building a Bandwagon: Women and Ideas

Enthusiasm matters a lot—enthusiasm and energy. And you must have faith in your idea; then you can face criticism honestly and move beyond it.

> Ruth Whitney—Editor-in-Chief, *Glamour*

If someone lets it die, you must be willing to pick up the pieces of your idea and put it back together. And you must be willing to transfer the responsibility for it to a place where it can be taken care of. A lot of ideas fall through for lack of follow-through.

> Cristine Candela—National President,
> Women's Equity Action League; former
> Special Assistant to the Chairman, U.S.
> Safety Products Commission

Springing a full-blown idea on people may be fun, but it's ill-advised. People may support you if you give them enough time to think about your ideas, enough time to climb on board.

> Joy Simonson—Executive Director,
> National Advisory Council on Women's
> Educational Programs; former National
> Chairwoman, National Association of
> Commissions on Women

Women's experience in volunteerism is invaluable. You learn how to move people along, how to lead them. You do not order, fire, or pay them. You have to persuade *them to your way of thinking.*

> Patricia S. Lindh—Vice President, The
> Bank of America; former Assistant to
> First Lady Betty Ford

You'd better be aware that the safest reaction people can give is, "No, I don't think it will work." I cannot think of ever having had an idea surface where everyone liked it. It's just so much easier, so much safer for people to say, "No, it won't work." Then you can't blame them if something doesn't work.

> Rep. Patricia Schroeder (D., Colorado)

At the point of putting an idea out to the public, be damned clear it is the best possible way to address that issue. If you are not, the minute

*you waver, people begin to sabotage and take potshots at you. Ulti-
mately, they may win; they may take control.*

> Audrey Rowe—Acting Administrator,
> Social Rehabilitation Administration,
> District of Columbia; former President,
> National Women's Political Caucus

*We began to talk about the idea, to say, "Wouldn't it be fun if we could
do our own thing?" The more we talked about it, the more exciting it
became. Timing was perfect, and the idea worked. Timing is critical!*

> Julia M. Walsh—Chairman of the Board,
> Julia M. Walsh and Sons, Inc. (Member,
> New York Stock Exchange)

What inspired these comments about ideas? Questions we
asked some of the nation's most innovative and successful
women. And where did we get *our* questions? From other
women, some new to management and others veterans of the
game.

To learn more about the business of bandwagon building, we
talked with nine women executives to explore their ideas about
ideas. We talked about generalities and specifics, about the ab-
stract and the concrete.

In talking with each of the women, we asked questions about
conceiving, developing, supporting, and selling ideas. We asked
about danger signs that would indicate that an idea or concept
is in trouble. Finally, we asked if female managers had skills or
problems in developing and selling ideas that were unique to
them.*

The nine women are among America's finest. They are successful, highly visible, enormously competent, recognized not
only as top professionals in their own fields but also as women

---

* "Unique to them," refers to women as a group of managers whose socialization and experience in the working world may have led to problems or opportunities that are more prevalent among women than men in the same positions.
There is no consideration here of *uniqueness* related to biological or physiological
characteristics!

who care about and promote fair treatment for women in the working world. Those who notice such things will observe that we made no effort to select one woman from academe, business, organizational life, the East Coast, the West Coast, and so on. Since the prerogative was ours and since we did not attempt to construct a scientific sample, we chose the women *we*, personally, wanted to include.

THE BEGINNINGS

We asked our bandwagon builders how they came up with their best ideas and how they knew that the ideas were, in fact, good.

Ruth Whitney talked about a very specific process, one that puts ideas into a track that ends on the pages of *Glamour* or in the wastebasket. "Here's an example. We wanted to do a spectacular in the December issue and came up with a 'calendar to save money by.' I set the ground rules for the idea in my own head, ideas about what I wanted to get out of that spectacular and who it should appeal to." Next, Ms. Whitney said she "set parameters, drawing a circle around the idea and describing the circle" for her art director and her managing editor. The idea was now established, isolated, and described. It was given an existence of its own.

"I test my ideas with my staff," she explained, "but I also have a lot of research that I can rely on. I get editorial research on every single page of every issue of *Glamour*. There's hardly an idea in the world that hasn't been researched." Ms. Whitney knows from her research reports just what her readers find interesting or not interesting or "sort of" interesting. Because she had seen reports that told her that the topics of saving money and inflation rated high in reader interest, she knew her idea was on the right track. A calendar for the new year combined with a sizzling topic—money—resulted in a marketable idea.

Does this mean that you must have access to an extensive in-house research service to test your ideas? Certainly not. Published research reports in local libraries tell what people are buying or not buying, where they are traveling, what they do for a living, how much money they spend on what kinds of activities. Readily available consumer reports are excellent research materials.

Margaret Adams at *Good Housekeeping* does what a lot of successful women do when they get an idea they hope is a great one. "I need to get away by myself and think it through before taking another step with it." With Ms. Adams, there is an interesting exercise that takes place when an idea has "caught fire" in her. "I trace its origin. And when I do, I usually find that it is something that has been with me for some time. Something, some need, has sparked the memory of a thought I have had for a long time." (We like the picture of filing away bits of creative genius and then pulling them out to fit new opportunities.)

Joy Simonson, whose specialty is women's education, offered some good words of advice about part of the process she uses during the conception of an idea. "I select people for those one-on-one discussions based on my feelings of trust and reliance. With those who are generally nonsupportive, those who aren't going to like *any* idea, I just don't make the effort."

Mulling an idea over for a few days, setting parameters for it, and then brainstorming with trusted colleagues seems to be a successful process. Representative Pat Schroeder believes that one must have that first "mulling" time, because "brainstorming at the very beginning is not all that productive. And then later, when you *do* brainstorm, when the idea has taken shape and you want to bounce it off a friend, you have to be willing to have other people dump all over your idea. You have to be as willing for that to happen as you are to have them say, 'What a terrific idea!'"

The bouncing-off process results, Audrey Rowe noted, in feedback that changes the original idea. "Almost always I incorporate others' thoughts into my original idea." She finds that she gets the best feedback by asking indirect questions, "questions that impact on the idea without telling what the idea is. I get far more objective answers that way," she said.

Is a manager always able to try new ideas? No, and if she is smart she will recognize limitations that may exist for her. Julia Walsh noted that the nature of the financial world is such that before she began her own organization she was quite reluctant to propose new ideas. "In that structure, the kind of role I played was fairly circumscribed by the way our business operates. The security . . . limited my willingness to step up and out and do anything really new and different."

Now of course, as head of her own firm, she is "at least able to throw ideas out to the group." If an idea fails? "I hope it doesn't; but if it does, I don't have to apologize for it."

Much can be said about the right to fail, most of which will not be said in these pages. If your role is such that it is possible for you to propose new ideas (and most of us fall into that category most of the time), do so. Before you do, however, make certain that you (1) give yourself some careful mulling-over time so that the idea is fairly well developed in your own mind, (2) establish parameters and a description for the idea, (3) consult some objective research that can reinforce your own feelings about the viability of the idea and that can sell others on it, and (4) test it out in friendly company.

GETTING SUPPORT

Once an idea is under way, how do you build support for it? How do you get people to step up onto your bandwagon?

Mary King of ACTION had a sure-fire answer. "Propose the idea to others in such a way that they think it is theirs, that they suggest you follow the course you already *know* you want to follow." Mary talked about the necessity to go beyond *endorsement* of ideas to *support* for them. Endorsement is passive; support is active.

Suppose the person whose support you need is one with whom you simply cannot communicate effectively? Ms. King suggested identifying someone else whom that person trusts, someone who also believes in your idea. Even though the idea is yours and the excitement is yours as well, she cautioned that "the best person to sell the idea is not always you."

Ruth Whitney believes that the process of building support for your bandwagon begins with the quality of that first explanation of what it is you're trying to do, why you think the problem needs to be solved now, and how you think your idea is going to solve it: a direct and orderly sales job. Audrey Rowe's technique is somewhat different, and more like Ms. King's. She tells those from whom she is seeking support that she *thinks* she *might* want to use this great idea, but is rather low key about it all. Ms. Rowe lets her audience develop the excitement, sell *her*, and, in fact, "become the brokers for the idea."

Sometimes an idea is so controversial that it requires a major selling campaign. When Congresswoman Schroeder came to the House of Representatives, she challenged the chairman of the Armed Services Committee and the system that protected his position. She believed she had a better idea. After more than a year of perseverance, she brought people around to her way of thinking and the system was changed. "It worked," she said, "but it was 18 months of real pain. It took constantly documenting, having a calm voice, talking to people, selling, persuading, convincing them that my ideas were sound."

What does Representative Schroeder's experience tell others? "You begin by making a tremendous commitment to the idea," she said. While it is important to recognize those times when opposition means that an idea must be abandoned, it is equally important to know when "to go to the mat" for what you believe is a sound idea.

Patricia Lindh, now a vice president of the world's largest bank, has had extensive experience with volunteers and some blue-ribbon political experience in the White House. Together these worlds taught her much about gaining support for ideas. "In volunteerism and in politics you have to know how to bring people around to your ideas. You learn a lot about persuasion." Ms. Lindh sees two very important prerequisites for persuasion. "You *must* have a good product or idea. And you must believe it is in the best interests of everyone."

A place where persuasion is a frequently needed tool is in a meeting. Meetings, it seems, have become a way of life in today's business world. It follows that a lot of gathering of support and selling of ideas take place in meetings. It also follows that this may be very dangerous ground, given normal competition among peers and given the fact that women can be preferred peer targets.

Cristine Candela of the Women's Equity Action League suggested extensive premeeting legwork. "I spend a lot of time on individual selling—one on one. If I *really* want something to go, something very important, I do a lot of selling long before I go into a meeting to discuss an idea."

Margaret Adams said she "hedges a little" in a meeting where people have been asked to bring in original ideas, their versions of someone else's idea, or ideas for a particular purpose. "I find myself sitting back, waiting for all the clouds to appear, blow up, evaporate or enlarge, confuse. Then I try to say, with as much honesty and directness as I can muster, whatever it is I have in my mind." She waits, it seems, for the dust to settle and for others to have their say.

Ms. Adams noted that even people "with the best ideas may be fearful about voicing them in a meeting." She advised that one "should rise up and speak with confidence in order to be *really* heard."

LETTING GO

At some point, it almost always is necessary to delegate some of the responsibility for selling your idea and bringing it to life. It means letting go. To do so may not be easy, and not everyone is able to manage the process gracefully.

Our bandwagon experts all believe in delegating, in letting go at the right time. Just when *is* the right time? That depends upon the particular idea, the environment in which it is germinating, and the staff resources available. Mary King said she starts delegating "immediately, once the strategy is developed.

The *sequence* [the manner in which her developmental steps will take place] is best figured out alone, but once the basics are down and the strategy set, I start delegating." As a result, Ms. King believes, "the strategy changes because of the chemistry of others and the addition of new people."

Teamwork is a working style that Margaret Adams enjoys, so she prefers to delegate to those she believes can work well as a team. "The best, most comfortable time for me is when I know that each person, whatever her job, is totally capable of doing that job and understanding the work of the others. This is the best of all possible worlds. If that's delegation, and I think it is, I love it!"

Pat Lindh suggested that on rare occasions one might not *want* to delegate. "Very seldom do I hang on when I should let go, but sometimes—just for the fun of it and when I am really enjoying something particularly—I will not delegate." This rare break with the rules seems okay to us. Every once in a while, when a manager can have fun with an idea, it is worth a great deal in terms of personal satisfaction and growth. And who says a manager can't have fun now and again?

Although delegation is a positive management tool, it can create problems—problems of process, not concept. "Delegating takes a lot of time. You have to think everything through to delegate. Sometimes it's the time factor—there's just not enough of it. You simply don't have *time* to delegate!" observed Ruth Whitney. Pat Schroeder, who said she delegates "a lot," warned that "nobody is going to care about your idea like you do—you have to follow up every single day."

Joy Simonson raised the problem of women entering a working environment from situations where they have been "bosses of their own domains." In this new environment they must "take orders from those above and get good performance from those below them. They may find it difficult to delegate and try instead to do everything themselves. I guess it's a 'Please, Mom, I'd rather do it myself' problem."

Let's consider delegation in a broader sense. Julia Walsh, in establishing her big idea—her own financial firm—offered an excellent example. "With us," she noted, "delegation in our new organization kind of fell into place. We had a mixture of people that permitted us to delegate without any real difficulty. We had all the pieces."

The lesson to be learned from the Walsh experience is a critical one: matching people to the right tasks. And *this* is delegation in the broader sense; it is important to understand its dynamics. It must be used in selling the bigger idea, which may be a new business or a significant new product or a financing package that will make you a million. Delegation means appointing someone to represent *your* interests. It means, as we have noted elsewhere, that you must allow that person to represent your interests fully; that is, you must delegate appropriate authority and adequate resources along with responsibility.

RECOGNIZING DANGER SIGNALS

Any idea run up the flagpole is going to get some potshots. Some may be justified, others may not. It is critical that you be able to distinguish people who are attempting to sink your idea because it is *yours* and not theirs from those who are offering legitimate criticism. Sometimes it isn't easy. Saboteurs come cleverly disguised.

Margaret Adams said she gets a very definite message if her pet idea receives a lot of early, strong objection. "If I get a lot of no's too soon, I know the idea is *damned* good." She believes that "some people involved in decisions about whether or not to buy your idea can be nonreceptive because they know the idea really *is* good." The opposite climate of opinion, she observed, is one "where people are informed and bright and not afraid—where they are, in fact, stirred by new ideas."

Joy Simonson warned that we must be "sufficiently open to legitimate responses or objections from other people. But we may be prone to focus so much on the *idea,* the *presentation,* and *ourselves* that we may not even notice the valid danger signals."

Audrey Rowe, who is a master at communications, feels that internal grapevines are essential to warding off sabotage that can kill your best idea. "You really can get good information from your informal network about trouble that may be brewing," she advised. "You can learn much about the processes of accepting, rejecting, or sabotaging through this kind of communication. There's not much that works better."

Mary King, along with Julian Bond, was in charge of communications for the Student Nonviolent Coordinating Committee in the early 1960s. During those years, threats to ideas could turn into threats to lives. Ms. King, by enhancing public awareness of these threats, worked to protect people, their ideas, and their rights to express them. This experience, unique to its time and place, taught her to anticipate hostility and to prepare for it.

For the most part, the women felt that even the best ideas may be subject to sabotage in our highly competitive world. Also, they reminded us that one must watch for signs of trouble and attempt to separate honest and valid criticism from that which is generated by small minds and/or vicious intent. Expect trouble, they said, but as Ms. King urged, "Don't be paranoid about it." Trouble may come from within or without—perhaps one is not as prepared as one might be, perhaps the idea is not researched well enough, or perhaps there is not enough experience to make it go. And even if there is, perhaps others perceive otherwise.

For Julia Walsh, signs of danger to her bandwagon were of a unique nature. And they came from inside. Ms. Walsh, whose fledgling firm initially had family members in all key management positions, felt that the *lack* of objective criticism was a real threat to the business. "We needed people who could be out there and say to us, 'Oh, that's a bunch of garbage.'" Fortunately, she noted, superb talent came to the firm almost immediately and "balance came with it. We had our criticism."

Take our word for it. If you aren't getting enough objective criticism, do something about it. And if you are getting too much criticism, it may be, as Margaret Adams told us, that your idea is terrific. It also may be, however, that your work has some real shortcomings. It is up to you to listen carefully, assess all the information, and find out.

SELLING YOURSELF

Is it as important to sell yourself as it is to sell your idea? "It's not important," Pat Lindh said, "it's essential!" The rest of our experts agreed.

But you may not have to sell yourself each time around. Ruth Whitney described a "climate of acceptance" which must exist if others are to treat you and your ideas objectively. She feels that she has that acceptance at *Glamour* and that, at this stage of her working life, "the idea is more important than the person." She added, "You must keep in mind that I've had this job for 11 or 12 years. When I first came, obviously I had to sell myself to *everybody*. But once you have a climate of acceptance, it's selling the idea that matters."

SOMETHING SPECIAL

Do women have skills or problems special to them that influence their ability to manage and, therefore, their ability to build bandwagons?

Margaret Adams: "Essentially there are no real differences in executives. Men come packaged poorly and women come packaged poorly. Men come packaged magnificently and women come packaged magnificently. Both can lie, cheat, steal, and charm. There are robber baronesses just as there are robber barons. And there are sainted men just as there are sainted women.

"But I will admit there are differences brought about by experience and socialization. Women simply haven't been aware that they must take charge of their own existence. Somehow, men are aware from birth that not much is ever going to come from a silver platter. Women must learn to take charge!"

209

Pat Lindh sees the woman executive as "walking through a thicket of preconceived ideas, most of which are subconsciously held. And since they *are* subconscious, they are difficult to combat. Women must work harder to demonstrate that they are competent, capable, ambitious, dedicated, and in it for the same reasons their male colleagues are."

The belief that women have special skills and perceptions exists among several of the bandwagon builders. "Women have much better people-management skills," Audrey Rowe said. "They are in tune to the dynamics of interpersonal relations and can perceive trouble spots and move to eliminate them."

Ms. Rowe also believes that women are "better organized thinkers" and so, "as managers, they think through how best to get from A to Z and what is necessary in between." Their special problems she sees as those society created. "We don't delegate enough; we try to do the whole job ourselves. We seem to feel we must *prove* that we can deliver!"

Cristine Candela said that she risked "sounding trite" when she raised the issue of women with growing-up experiences based on individual rather than competitive performance, or discussed the fact that women have not learned to pursue ideas and work in teams the way men have. "Most work as individuals in their approach. We tend to pursue our goals in a more isolated fashion.

"But," she said, "I do not denigrate at all the characteristics women bring into the business world. Their ways will result in a pattern that is more humanistic, one which will be to the advantage of the business community and to productivity in general."

Ruth Whitney believes that "women have better antennae. They can sense things, have grown up trying to sense things, and I think they are good at it. I think often that a woman in a group situation has a clearer picture of *all* the things that are happening in the situation. Maybe she's working harder at it."

"I think women lack some skills because of lack of experience," Julia Walsh observed. "I found the risks involved in being on my own were something I had to work to adapt to—borrowing money, 'leveraging,' making certain kinds of decisions." She

210

said that if anyone had told her all of this would have been difficult when she was first on her own, she would have said, "It's not possible. Not me."

She has conquered these difficult feelings now but would like, when time permits, to discuss them with a male counterpart who has undergone the same kind of experience. Given everything, Ms. Walsh said, "My tendency is to think that . . . if I were a man, I wouldn't have felt that way!"

Mary King sees women as good managers except for one area: conflict resolution. "The cultural norms for women in a conflict situation call for submission, avoidance, withdrawal—none of these is appropriate for a manager." However, she added, "Women are wonderful at diagnosis, at seeing the roadblocks. Their personal diagnostic abilities give them real strength as managers."

In summary, women who are creative, who are responsible for nurturing and selling their ideas, seem to have some very definite thoughts about how to take an idea from conception to the marketplace. They believe in a careful thinking-through process, objective testing, sharing responsibility for development of the idea, being on the look-out for signs that their ideas are in trouble. And they believe, for the most part, that their ideas will sell only when "buyers" have a goodly measure of confidence not only in the ideas but also in those who conceive them. And lastly, they agree that, because of socialization and a business world that still treats women differently from men, female managers have some advantages—and some disadvantages—in the "idea game."

Most importantly, they suggest that *process* is important, a process based on objectivity and the knowledge that competition is keen. We believe the process is especially helpful when a record is kept of each attempt to sell a substantive idea, when notes remind us of what worked and what did not. Success, it seems, is a habit. And, as Aristotle told us, habit can be learned.

22. Management Skills Assessment
A Personal Assessment of Understandings, Preferences, and Skills

ARE YOU a good manager? Are you an organizer, a planner, an evaluator? Do you derive real pleasure from the constant day-to-day contact that comes with managing people? What management capabilities do you know you have? Think you have? Know you do not have? Wish you had?

You must have certain abilities related to management if success in the executive suite is your goal. It's a wise woman who knows whether she has these or, at least, attempts to find out.

What follows are some questions about understandings, preferences, and skills related to management. They are important to you if you are a manager, intend to be one someday, or are on your way from one management level to another. Some of them require you to draw conclusions that may be difficult—

you may not be able to assess yourself objectively if there is little evidence to support your self-assessment. Still, it *is* worth the effort to try to identify those areas in which you need additional experience or knowledge. Where the evidence is apparent, you will be able to note areas of competence, and this, too, is helpful.

Note that there are five response columns for the assessment that follows. The first, A, indicates that you *know* the answer is yes. For example, you *know* you can manage a budget because you have done so. Column B indicates that, in all honesty, you *think* the answer is yes, but really don't know. Take our budget example. You know you have successfully managed certain monitoring activities but have not had the full responsibility yourself. In your opinion, the likelihood is that you would be able to do so. Check Column B. Mark Column C if you simply do not know the answer. You may be able to do what is asked; on the other hand, you may not. Column D indicates a definite no. You have tried to handle the problem of budget control and simply cannot do it. This is a management activity that is beyond your ability or your interest. In addition, check Column E when you find something you want to identify for improvement.

The set of questions ranges widely by design. It should help you to look at a variety of considerations from several perspectives. It asks for conclusions sometimes and at other times does not. We think it is an unusual and helpful mixture. Give it a try.

After you have made your assessment, how should the results be analyzed? First of all, there is no magic number of "yes, I know," responses that will guarantee success. Secondly, the assessment must be thought of as just what it is—a means of identifying strengths and weaknesses. No number of Column A answers less Column D answers balanced by Column B earns the key to the executive suite. It is recommended that the assessment be made next year and every few years afterward to measure progress in your own growth and development as a manager.

	A Yes, I know.	B Yes, I think.	C Don't know.	D No.	E Improve!

Planning, organizing, controlling, making decisions

1. Do you keep abreast of changes in economic, technological, industrial, social, and political conditions which can affect your area or kind of business?

2. Can you formulate goals and objectives as a basis for the work and direction of a unit of activity?

3. Can you develop long- and short-range strategies to meet goals and objectives? Can you express all these elements in the context of a written plan to guide organizational activities?

4. Are you careful to include an evaluation mechanism in the planning for every project, activity, or product?

5. Can you prepare an operating budget for a significant area of activity (department/division/product)?

6. Are you able to restrict spending to prescribed limits? Does your *record* show this ability?

7. Do you believe that employee performance should be guided and measured by reasonable,

achievable, mutually agreed-upon, and objective performance standards? Do you practice that belief?

8. Can you accept the fact that, because of political realities, some things just won't work?

9. Can you set priorities? Can you rank competing tasks according to priority criteria?

10. Can you manage and organize your time? Can you keep on schedule?

11. Do you establish operating policies for yourself and your unit whether or not your organization requires you to do so?

12. Can you delegate responsibility and *authority* appropriately and comfortably?

13. When you delegate to others, can you let go of the reins and give them an opportunity to maneuver?

14. Do you understand problem-solving methodologies?

15. Do you apply your knowledge of problem-solving processes to real-life situations?

16. Do you have the ability to define, explain, and/or clarify difficult or complex issues to others?

17. Are you willing to make tough decisions?

	A Yes, I know.	B Yes, I think.	C Don't know.	D No.	E Improve!

Communicating, relating, responding

18. Do you make a conscious effort to communicate directly, openly, and honestly with everyone around you?

19. Do you have an orderly process for handling communications that come to your office?

20. When you listen, do you really *apply* yourself to hearing what the other person is saying?

21. Are you aware of the "vocabulary" of nonverbal communication—of body language?

22. Are you hooked into and able to use to advantage your organization's formal communications system?

23. Are you hooked into an informal communications system *by your own choosing?*

24. Can you recognize communications gaps in an organization? Do you know how to begin correcting them?

25. Do you have confidence in your business writing skills?

26. Are you skillful at making verbal presentations? When your presentation is completed, do the

questions you receive indicate that you have gotten your message across?

27. Before entering a negotiation session, do you know what terms you will not give up, those you are willing to give up, and those you are willing to use for bargaining purposes?

28. In a mediation role, are you able to listen supportively, interpret well, and help others understand varying points of view?

29. If you feel confident about someone, are you able to *display* that confidence and trust?

30. Are you generally diplomatic in your relationships and dealings with others? Is this evidenced by others' references to your tact and sensitivity?

31. Do you act quickly, decisively, and *carefully* in solving unanticipated problems (as opposed to shooting from the hip)?

32. Are you unflappable in emergencies? In politically sticky or uncomfortable situations?

Leading, motivating, innovating, exploring

33. Can you plan for and effect change?

34. Are you willing to take reasonable risks?

35. Can you work without frequent supervision or reinforcement from higher-ups?

36. Does being a *little* overextended motivate you?

	A	B	C	D	E
	Yes, I know.	Yes, I think.	Don't know.	No.	Improve!
37. Do you have the respect of your peers, subordinates, superiors?					
38. Do you enjoy being a leader and assuming major responsibilities for directing the work and activities of others?					
39. Do you know the difference between power and authority? Can you use each effectively?					
40. Do you feel comfortable chairing a committee, group, or task force? Do you believe others see you as a skillful chairperson?					
41. Do you empathize rather than sympathize?					
42. Do you respect others' values?					
43. Do you attempt to *motivate* others through carefully thought-out techniques?					
44. Are you generally able to persuade others to your point of view?					
45. Do you seek ideas and recommendations from your staff as an integral part of your decision-making process?					
46. Do you generally use reward or incentives rather than threats or fear to motivate others?					

47. Do you believe most people have imagination, ingenuity, and creativity?
48. Do you look for hidden potential in people? In programs or projects? In markets? In systems?
49. Do you look for new ways to do things?
50. Do you look for new things to *do*? Are you willing to pioneer? To be the first? To experiment?

23. Do What Scares You the Most

O, the days that are gone by
O, the days that are no more;
When my eye was bold and fearless
And my hand was on the oar.

    The Wasps
    (Tr. Richard Cumberland)

WHEN YOUR hand is on the oar your passengers have a right to expect you to get them through the storm rather than return to port whenever rainclouds appear. Especially so, when those rainclouds are created of your own fears—fears that may be keeping you from doing your job to the best of your ability. To analyze yourself and the impact of fear on your performance, ask: What do I fear the most, and what effect does fear have on how well I do my job?

There is no getting around it. If fear keeps you from performing well, forget about moving up in management.

The purpose of the following exercise is to help you identify typical professional fears that may be barriers to your success as a senior manager.

PART I

On a scale of 1 to 10, rate yourself on each of the following questions. In other words, decide what places on the scale best describe your fear level if you are faced with the described tasks. No one will be looking over your shoulder (we assume), so be honest.

NO FEAR   SCARED STIFF
How afraid are you to. . .

1. 1   2   3   4   5   6   7   8   9   10
   Fire someone?

2. 1   2   3   4   5   6   7   8   9   10
   Take a job as a top administrator of a large organization?

3. 1   2   3   4   5   6   7   8   9   10
   Give a major speech to a large audience?

4. 1   2   3   4   5   6   7   8   9   10
   Arrange a meeting with the governor, the head of the American Broadcasting Company (ABC), or any other power source?

5. 1   2   3   4   5   6   7   8   9   10
   Ask for a raise you think you deserve?

6. 1   2   3   4   5   6   7   8   9   10
   Travel to strange places alone?

7. 1   2   3   4   5   6   7   8   9   10
   Attend an important meeting as your organization's sole representative?

8. 1   2   3   4   5   6   7   8   9   10
   Hire someone whose fine talents could be threatening to your own job security?

9. 1   2   3   4   5   6   7   8   9   10
   Take a vacation and leave an assistant in charge?

10. 1   2   3   4   5   6   7   8   9   10
    Go to court over an important issue?

11. | 1 | 2 | 3 | 4 | 5 | 6 | 7 | 8 | 9 | 10 |

Undergo a tough evaluation of your performance on the job?

12. | 1 | 2 | 3 | 4 | 5 | 6 | 7 | 8 | 9 | 10 |

Meet with a hostile group?

13. | 1 | 2 | 3 | 4 | 5 | 6 | 7 | 8 | 9 | 10 |

Do a live TV or radio interview?

14. | 1 | 2 | 3 | 4 | 5 | 6 | 7 | 8 | 9 | 10 |

Entertain business associates in your home, club, a restaurant, etc.?

15. | 1 | 2 | 3 | 4 | 5 | 6 | 7 | 8 | 9 | 10 |

Perform a thorough evaluation of your staff's performance on the job?

16. | 1 | 2 | 3 | 4 | 5 | 6 | 7 | 8 | 9 | 10 |

Go through an interview for an important job?

17. | 1 | 2 | 3 | 4 | 5 | 6 | 7 | 8 | 9 | 10 |

Take a job as head of an organization whose workers are, for the most part, considerably older than you?

18. | 1 | 2 | 3 | 4 | 5 | 6 | 7 | 8 | 9 | 10 |

Accept a job where you supervise only men?

19. | 1 | 2 | 3 | 4 | 5 | 6 | 7 | 8 | 9 | 10 |

Accept a job where you supervise only women?

20. | 1 | 2 | 3 | 4 | 5 | 6 | 7 | 8 | 9 | 10 |

Ask your boss, board, or partners for a month's leave to return to school?

21. | 1 | 2 | 3 | 4 | 5 | 6 | 7 | 8 | 9 | 10 |

Travel for business reasons with a male coworker or boss for one week or longer?

22. | 1 | 2 | 3 | 4 | 5 | 6 | 7 | 8 | 9 | 10 |

Accept a job which is so complex you know at the outset that proficiency and confidence are at least a year away?

23. | 1 | 2 | 3 | 4 | 5 | 6 | 7 | 8 | 9 | 10 |

Confront a subordinate about her inferior work performance?

222

Do What Scares You the Most

24. | 1 | 2 | 3 | 4 | 5 | 6 | 7 | 8 | 9 | 10 |
Confront a competent but tough-minded subordinate about a single incident of work behavior of which you do not approve?

25. | 1 | 2 | 3 | 4 | 5 | 6 | 7 | 8 | 9 | 10 |
Be visible on the job or in the community?

26. | 1 | 2 | 3 | 4 | 5 | 6 | 7 | 8 | 9 | 10 |
Hear criticism of your work?

27. | 1 | 2 | 3 | 4 | 5 | 6 | 7 | 8 | 9 | 10 |
Have fun in your job?

28. | 1 | 2 | 3 | 4 | 5 | 6 | 7 | 8 | 9 | 10 |
Make your office reflect your executive status?

29. | 1 | 2 | 3 | 4 | 5 | 6 | 7 | 8 | 9 | 10 |
Let the buck stop at your desk when the issue is a controversial one?

30. | 1 | 2 | 3 | 4 | 5 | 6 | 7 | 8 | 9 | 10 |
Be labeled a "women's-libber" by standing up for individual rights when you see a wrong?

31. | 1 | 2 | 3 | 4 | 5 | 6 | 7 | 8 | 9 | 10 |
Meet with a very important person whom you've only heard about and never met?

32. | 1 | 2 | 3 | 4 | 5 | 6 | 7 | 8 | 9 | 10 |
Invest, spend, or commit large sums of money?

33. | 1 | 2 | 3 | 4 | 5 | 6 | 7 | 8 | 9 | 10 |
Show anger?

34. | 1 | 2 | 3 | 4 | 5 | 6 | 7 | 8 | 9 | 10 |
Speak up at important meetings?

35. | 1 | 2 | 3 | 4 | 5 | 6 | 7 | 8 | 9 | 10 |
(Your pet fear—your personal/professional bogeyperson)

PART II

Count the number of test questions where you gave yourself a rating on the fear scale of 6 or above. If your count was—

- 1 to 7, consider yourself fairly well self-assured and experienced in tough situations. Congratulations.
- 8 to 17, recognize that your overall fear level is probably causing you some management problems—problems which may be perceived by your staff and others.
- 18 or more, you have a great deal to work on! Take time to analyze your fears. Is it authority figures? Hostile situations? Conflict? Your personal security? Your professional security? Fear of being disliked? (See May the good Lord take a liking to you because not everyone will, "Maxims to Operate and Succeed By.") Doubt of your own intelligence or competence? Whatever the answers are, consider this: "What is the worst thing that could happen to me if I plunged forward and did every task I've checked?"

PART III

Of the items with a fear rating of 6 or above, note which fears have caused you to avoid taking action in the past or may keep you from taking action in the future. Review your answers until it becomes apparent which fears must be overcome if you want to develop strength and confidence.

PART IV

Those items with a high fear rating that have not kept you from taking action are a fairly good indication of fears that do not inhibit your actions, even though you may dread facing the situations. Evidently you have been practicing the magic of doing what scares you the most. Keep up the practice and surprise yourself with what you really can do when timidity and counterproductive trepidation are barriers of the past.

24. Do You Know Where You're Going?

For 10 years now, Susan has been sitting at the same midlevel manager's desk. Every year, she has announced that "this is my last year here. I'm going to move on soon, maybe to school, maybe to another company, maybe to my own business." But she never leaves. She just remains on the curb, watching the parade go by, saying to herself, "Sooner or later, I'll be discovered and get my reward."

Margaret also has been at her same manager's spot for 10 years. She, too, wants to move on, but she prefaces her comments with, "Joe said he would find me a better job, but as usual, he hasn't come through." She's a perpetual Cinderella, always waiting for a Prince Charming to bail her out of her misery.

Jan is different, still. Nearly every two or three years she has

225

had some top project receive statewide or national attention; she's landed some good top-management jobs with various organizations; she always seems busy and involved. But Jan has managed herself by the Ping-Pong-ball/mousetrap technique. No one can discern a pattern to her career behavior as the traps are randomly set off by bouncing balls. She aimlessly bolts from one job to another, having no idea where it is all leading.

Most of us set goals for our businesses. We know the payoffs of a well-defined organizational direction. The same should be true for our own business careers. We need to take charge there, too. We need to get out of the maze and design our own paths leading to rewards *we* want for ourselves.

Managers can leave their career development to luck. Some do, and for all we know they may be very successful. However, based on our work as career-goal consultants and speakers, we believe that most female managers do not want to rely on lady luck; they prefer to rely on careful planning. There is a recognition that the best do not *always* rise to the top like cream, that hard work and competence do not *always* result in a promotion, that being gifted and talented in management does not *always* guarantee discovery in the boardroom and immediate stardom.

The ultimate goal of career planning is, of course, to head toward those things that make one happy in one's working and personal lives. Perhaps it takes money, advancement, an exciting environment, peer recognition, or a number of other good things. Our job is to help you make some of those decisions and to record them in such a way that you can evaluate your progress toward your career goals.

LOOKING AT YOUR CAREER ANCHORS

As you contemplate what the contents of your career plan should be, perhaps this short exercise will help you understand more clearly what it is you're looking for in your work.

Given all the choices you could have about changing jobs, moving to a new location, being promoted, going out on your own, moving from one company to another, working for this boss or that, what is it that you *will not give up?* What set of motivations, values, or attitudes have been guiding you or holding you in your career path? What are the career anchors that pull you back if you stray too far from what you want? Can you identify what is unchanging in your life so you can deal better with career decisions you need to make?

The concept of career anchors emerges from a lengthy and continuing study of graduate school alumni from the Sloan School of Management at the Massachusetts Institute of Technology. Edgar H. Schein, in his report of the findings of this study, lists five common anchor categories that reveal what a person fundamentally is looking for in a career. These anchors describe how a person perceives her own talents, needs, and values based on early work experiences. They help an individual tie together and give meaning to her work.*

Read through Schein's descriptions of career anchors and see which self-concept most nearly describes what you feel you would not give up if forced to make a choice. Then go back and decide which *one* category best describes what you would be least willing to give up in your work. You may wish to use the information in later exercises in this chapter.

ANCHOR 1: MANAGERIAL COMPETENCE

This person wants a position of responsibility and one where her managerial skills make a difference. The most important components of this concept are:

1. *Analytical competence*—the ability to identify, analyze, and solve problems under conditions of incomplete information and uncertainty.
2. *Interpersonal competence*—the ability to influence, supervise, lead, manipulate, and control people at all levels of the organization toward the more effective achievement of organizational goals.

* Edgar H. Schein, *Career Dynamics* (Reading, Mass.: Addison-Wesley, 1978).

3. *Emotional competence*—the capacity to be stimulated by emotional and interpersonal crises rather than exhausted or debilitated by them, the capacity to bear high levels of responsibility without becoming paralyzed, and the ability to exercise power without guilt or shame.

ANCHOR 2: TECHNICAL/FUNCTIONAL COMPETENCE

People with this need are generally motivated by the challenge of the technical work they do, not by the managerial role they may have. If a member of this group holds supervisory responsibility, she is usually supervising others in the same technical area, and she makes it clear that it is the area, not the supervising, that gives her motivation.

ANCHOR 3: SECURITY

These people, it is assumed, have an underlying need for security. They seek to stabilize their careers by linking themselves to given organizations. Generally, they allow the organization to define and manage their career. Their private aspirations appear to become secondary. Security-oriented individuals may change companies, but, chances are, there will be strong similarities between the organizations and job slots they go into. These individuals may also be quite willing to give up some autonomy in their careers to stabilize their life situation, such as taking jobs in only one community so that a family is not uprooted.

ANCHOR 4: CREATIVITY

These individuals are entrepreneurs: they want to create their own service, product, or organization through their own creative efforts. They want to express their business and managerial skills by building their own enterprises.

ANCHOR 5: AUTONOMY AND INDEPENDENCE

Members of this group want to lead their own lives in their own way and pursue whatever they choose in a self-determined fashion. They find organizational life to be restrictive, irrational, or intrusive into their private lives. They differ from entrepreneurs in that they are not preoccupied with building something; they simply want to be on their own.

INVENTORYING CAREER DESIRES

As a prelude to the final career goal plan, we've found that it pays to do a quick and uninhibited inventory of things a person enjoys doing in her work life or things a person *would like* to do at some time in her career. This quick brainstorming method of listing has several purposes: (1) it reinforces an individual's ideas about those aspects of her career she enjoys and may want to keep; (2) if she dares to dream, it brings out desires a person may have been suppressing because she has considered them unattainable; (3) it provides a format for quickly listing career likes without going into a lot of complicated detail; (4) it encourages women to look at desires in a *career* rather than in one specific *job*.

DIRECTIONS

On a sheet of paper, write down the numbers from 1 to 21 (see sample table that follows). Begin making a list of the 21 things you like to do in your work or things you would like to do or have happen sometime in your career. Do not worry about order of preference. Write anything that comes to mind; do not avoid your dreams.

Some items may be simple likes, while others could be major

229

desires that will take years to meet. Don't worry about having too many of one or the other. For now, jot down your ideas as they come to you.

Don't be surprised if you include an item that relates more to your personal than career life. It depends on the individual, but often it is difficult to completely separate the two. (Example: I want to have a business where my children or spouse can feel free to drop in during working hours.) Sometimes these desires serve as a definite guide to career decisions.

Be as specific as you can. If one of your desires is to make lots of money, put down how much. If you say you want to be a success, list what characteristic, if met, would tell you that you are.

Fill in all 21 spaces! It forces you to recall grandiose ideas as well as simple pleasures you want in your career.

When your list is done, make seven columns beside each number (see the table illustrated). Give the columns the following headings:

A. High, medium, or low interest
B. Those things that cost $1,000 or more to do
C. Those things that require you to acquire more skills
D. Those things that require you to live or work in a different company or geographical location in order to accomplish them
E. The approximate date you last engaged in or worked toward each desire
F. Those things that will be on your list 5 to 10 years from now
G. Those things that you could do over the next year or two

Complete the table by indicating which conditions (column heads) apply to each of your desires.

ANALYSIS

A. *High, medium, or low interest.* This activity encourages you to place some type of priority on your desires.

List career desires below. Be specific.	A. High, Medium, or Low Interest	B. $1,000 or More to Do	C. Need More Skills	D. Change Location	E. Date Last Worked Toward	F. 5–10 Years from Now	G. Can Do Next One or Two Years
1.							
2							
3							
4							
5							
etc.							

B. *$1,000 or more.* This helps you determine if you really need as much money as you thought in order to accomplish what you want. It could also tell you if you need to get in gear and earn more if you're really sincere about moving ahead on some ideas.

C. *Need more skills.* Activity in this column aids you in looking realistically at skills or credentials you may have to obtain before you can realize your goal. It's also a step toward putting desires into action. If you have a great many checks in this column, perhaps you will have to embark on a very rigid schedule of training if you want to reach your desires in a reasonable and acceptable length of time.

D. *Change location.* In terms of maintaining or meeting your career desires, a change in your place of work or geographic location may be highly desirable. Answers in this column also may reveal that you have *misled* yourself into believing you have to move to a different state or city to get what you want. Take time to analyze this one carefully! Have you been excessively loyal to the company at the expense of furthering your own career and happiness? If you have known you should make a move for a long time, what's been holding you back? Are you willing to take the possible risks involved with uprooting?

E. *Date last worked toward desires listed.* Your answers should be quite revealing when compared to the High, Medium, or Low Interest column. For example, if you have taken little action on items of high interest, chances are you aren't doing what you really want to do. Perhaps something or someone else has been controlling your life instead of you! If you've worked toward very few of your 21 desires over the last year, this may indicate that you are in a rut and need to take a little action before you get too lethargic.

F. *On list 5–10 years from now.* Ideally, you should have several desires marked in this column. This indicates that you have some long-term goals toward which to focus your immediate energies. However, if the items marked are *only* those things you hope to *maintain*, you'll want to recognize that you've stopped planning for yourself; that you're locked into one path that may not include alternatives in case the world does not stand still. There's more to consider than yourself out there.

G. *Those things that you could do over the next year or two.* If most of your 21 items have a check in this column, you are likely doing very little long-range planning. It may indicate that you haven't taken time to think about how your present activities can be used as building blocks for a better payoff in the future. In addition, you may be so short term in your thinking that you'll not be able to identify warnings of career barriers down the road. On the other hand, a moderate number of items that you could do over the next few years indicates that you have probably broken down some larger goals into specific and reachable action steps.

Think for a moment about what your answers tell you. Did you discover anything new about yourself? Have you taken control of your career? Are you just thinking about a job instead of a career? Can you see where great risks are facing you if you go ahead with some of your desires? Can you overcome them, and are you willing to deal with the consequences if it means moving your family, doing more travel, going back to school? Are you motivated enough to put your unmet desires into action? Use this exercise as a basis for your career plan on the next few pages.

DEVELOPING A CAREER PLAN

The purpose of a career plan is to list work-related goals that have a time line attached to them in order to guide you toward the best use of your talents, skills, and work efforts. The planning does not have to be complicated. However, it should be carefully considered. We suggest you begin with 5- to 10-year targets, and then work your way down to some concrete 1- or 2-year activities. You might want to use the following format for a guide.

Goal review and evaluation should take place at least once a year. A review refreshes your memory as to where you want to head and also allows you the chance to make changes in your direction if circumstances demand it.

MANAGEMENT STRATEGIES FOR WOMEN

1	2	3	4
Things to accomplish in 5–10 years.	Estimated date to accomplish goals in Column 1.	Steps needed in the next 1 or 2 years to do things in Column 1.	Definite date by when each step will be accomplished in Column 3.

Perhaps some risks have materialized in the kind of job, route, or goal you were heading toward and you need to provide an alternative for yourself. Perhaps you have met all your targets a little early and need to step up your action to keep on the move. Perhaps you have gotten so involved in your *job* that you have forgotten to implement some *career* steps.

25. How to Be Pregnant in the Executive Suite

WELCOME THE stork, but beware of the vulture that may not be far behind. While it is unpleasant to contemplate, it is a fact of life in the executive suite that *some* colleagues may try to take advantage of a pregnant female manager's perceived vulnerability. Others simply may become nuisances. Typical problem behavior includes:

- Attempting to take away important duties or opportunities because they are "just too demanding for the little-mother-to-be."
- Patronizing, overprotecting, mothering (or fathering); in all, perpetuating the myth that pregnant women are frail and sick.
- Refusing to go along with plans of the LMTB (little-mother-to-be) because "she probably won't be returning anyway"; using other delay and destroy tactics.

MANAGEMENT STRATEGIES FOR WOMEN

- Fussing over her, patting shoulder and tummy, clucking and cooing, and generally driving her bananas—especially when these things are done by subordinates and superiors who are getting too close and too personal.
- Refusing to follow directions from her (if she's their boss) because they consider her a lame duck. They believe that *all* women workers who become pregnant will be gone for months and months or will quit work altogether.

We have some suggestions on how to deal with these birds, understanding as we do that not all of them are acting out of evil intent. Some honestly believe that LMTBs are just one step this side of absent-minded foolishness, in ill health, and in need of protection. We also have some suggestions about ways to maintain your super-sharp executive appearance and wonderful air of confidence.

1. Don't announce the big event at work until you are ready to take control of the reactions to your announcement.
2. Make up your mind as soon as possible about working after the baby is born. Your decision will affect the willingness of employees and supervisors to support long-range plans and decisions.
3. Decide how much leave time you want both before and after the baby's arrival. Know your company and legal options. Assess your job responsibilities to determine how long the place can get along without you (it can, you know), or how long it would take others to usurp your authority should they desire.
4. Don't ask for special privileges unless you or your doctor feel they are really necessary.
5. Don't take foolish risks. Don't risk the baby's health or yours just to demonstrate that being pregnant cannot slow down a tiger like you.
6. Schedule medical appointments on your own time. Dispel the myth that pregnant employees are part-time workers.
7. No one likes a complainer. Keep your discomfort to yourself.

If it's all too much, have your secretary hold all calls; then, elevate your feet and take a snooze for 10 to 15 minutes.* Make her promise not to tell.

8. Continue to dress like an executive. Don't look like a pregnant Holly Hobby doll, a possibility if you fall for some of the typical maternity duds. Also, avoid the overnight campout look; baggy socks, pants, and nondescript or cutesie T-shirt tops make it psychologically difficult for people to view you as a serious manager. Grin and bear the cost of some slick-looking garments that can grow with you. It will help your feelings about *yourself* as well as others' feelings about you.

9. Make a *detailed* work plan to cover required activities while you are away. Set deadlines and fiscal parameters (factor a 10 percent leeway if possible, but keep this a secret), assign responsibilities, and outline reporting procedures. Make certain you go over the plan carefully with your full staff; copy the boss, the fiscal officer, and anyone else with a need to know. Have the boss (if you have one) sign off on the plan. Your careful planning, shared with the top executives, will impress them and earn you some important pluses for your skillful management.

10. Formulate some interim operating policies to serve as guidelines while you are away. If they are comprehensive and reasonable, there should be little that can happen to leave your staff wondering what to do when the unexpected occurs. Designate a deputy to serve for a specified period of time. With that person, do any reassigning of tasks necessitated by your absence and her extra responsibilities. (Some managers share this top assignment among several supervisors. The disadvantage is that *nobody* is really responsible for anything that goes right or wrong. The buck passes at satellite speed and never comes to rest. If you want to give all the key supervisors a chance at the helm, do so on different occasions, or have a number of pregnancies. Otherwise, one pregnancy, one deputy.) *Delegate sufficient interim authority to accompany interim re-*

---

* Daytime sleepiness can become a real problem. Your body may be giving you a signal that you need more rest. Or you may be getting adequate rest and still be suffering from drowsiness. It helps to schedule some stimulating activity or meeting during the time of the day when you usually get sleepy. Keeping active keeps your mind off the sleepies.

sponsibility. One cannot work without the other, and when you give your deputy the reins, give her both of them. If you try to hang onto one, she won't go forward; she'll go in a circle.

Once you have had your baby and are heading back to work, there are several things to consider if you are planning to breast-feed. For instance, setting a goal for the number of months you want to breastfeed your baby will make you more relaxed and will provide motivation on days when job pressures are heavy.

Think through the ramifications of nursing in your office. There are those individuals who will encourage you to bare your breast there, and those who will faint at the thought. We recommend that breastfeeding take place outside your office and in a private setting, given the need for others to concentrate on your work performance rather than on your personal bravado/courage/indecency/whatever.

If you nurse only in the morning and evening, express your breasts privately over the noon hour and store the milk in the refrigerator or a cooler in your desk. (Milk can be frozen for use while you are on travel. Also, starting baby early with formula now and again helps with scheduling problems.) If you choose to nurse at noon, find a sitter near the office whose home you can go to over the lunch hour. If you want to continue to nurse while traveling, take a sitter along. It's not as difficult as it sounds and may give you an emotional boost.

26. Standards and Values

TOP EXECUTIVES need to operate from an established set of standards and values.

Why? Because managers are busy people and need a strong philosophical base to help them make rapid decisions that are of quality and value. Because employees will often waste executives' time by bringing them less-than-superior reports or products if they don't know what is expected of them. Because managers are the leaders and are ultimately responsible for the quality of an organization. Because values and standards serve as a basis for comparison in measuring quality. Because high standards and values make an organization more desirable and useful. Because some things just should not be compromised if an executive wants a top-notch company or organization.

How *do* you establish a set of standards and values for yourself and your organization? Perhaps the first step is to make a list of those beliefs, qualities, and practices that *you* feel should not be compromised by yourself or your organization.

To help you do this, we have provided you with a sampling of general standard and value statements that we believe are important. Make note of those items with which you agree. Also, you will want to add to this list (at least mentally) any other statements that come to mind and that are germane to your circumstances. Keep asking yourself questions like these: Is there any area in which I need a stranger philosophical base to help make more rapid or higher quality decisions? Can I begin to define some now? How will I know if my organization is one of high quality? Not every situation which I may encounter can be foreseen but what fundamental ethical principles should be always present to guide me in my conduct?

1. *Accuracy.* Make it a habit; make it a particular concern in fiscal and public information areas.
2. *Acronyms.* Discourage use of them in front of the public or anyone else you suspect may be unfamiliar with the terms. It may seem like a small point, but why confuse or annoy others simply because they missed the meaning of your pet acronym? Save the F.U.F.F.U.A.A.* (frequently used and fairly frequently used acronyms and abbreviations) for shop talk only!
3. *Auditors.* They're bothersome but necessary for a good check-and-balance system. Give them all the information they request, but let them do the audit work or you won't get your own job done. And don't get uptight over every question they ask. If you've been running a clean operation, you have nothing to worry about. If they discover a few errors, you'd want to know about them anyway.
4. *Budgets.* Learn everything you can about the basics of budgeting and accounting. Even if you have the best budget officer in the world, remember the budget is *your* responsibility. Budget plans *must* be drawn carefully and appropriately; budgets *must* be controlled firmly and impeccably. (See "Avoiding Tooth-Fairy Economics.")

* Actual name of a Federal document.

240

5. *Canning people.** Sometimes it has to be done! Think about it. . . Would you like to have that person taking home a paycheck if you owned the outfit and saw illegal, unethical, or little work done? And don't let transfers to another department be your easy way out.

6. *Cheating (annual and sick leave, overtime).* Don't do it. It isn't fair. Use yourself as an example for others to follow.

7. *Clamming up.* When you are told something in confidence, keep it to yourself. Many a business situation has been beached because someone couldn't shut his mouth.

8. *Complaints.* Deal honestly with complaints, complainers, and the complained about. Demand documentation or justification. Don't accept idle gossip disguised as a valid complaint.

9. *Concern.* Treat the people who work for you with concern, respect, and consideration. Understand their humanness. They are not machines which will, with a drop or two of oil, hum along efficiently. Nor are they easily disposed of in a trash barrel if they break down.

10. *Conferences.* Usually a waste of time unless every agenda item is well planned, gutsy, and not of the garden club variety. Consult your conscience before holding one or sending an employee to one. (See "Creative Conferences.")

11. *Conference speakers.* Select the best. Avoid putting others on the program just to keep from hurting feelings. It's a waste of money to pay for their expenses and a waste of time to sit and listen to the bores. (See "Creative Conferences.")

12. *Contractors.* Use them when feasible rather than hiring full-time staff, or you'll find yourself spending the next few years trying to figure out ways to get rid of the extras or to keep them busy after the project ends. Caution! In the public sector, keep the bidding process competitive and open. Where possible and legal, give priority consideration to female and minority contractors.

13. *Decoration of office.* If you are in the public sector, buy your own personal decorative office items. The public will not furnish your home, so why should they go beyond the essentials for your office? If you're in the private sector, go to it—that sometimes is one of the advantages of being there!

14. *Ethics.* You better have your own code of high standards for your behavior. If you are in government service, the public will not

* Canning, in this case, as opposed to preserving.

tolerate a violation of their rights and, frankly, is skeptical about the desire of bureaucrats to meet citizen needs. Demonstrate your standards through your own conduct. Honesty, caring, and hard work have to start somewhere. It can help to narrow the credibility gap. If you are in the private sector, ethics means dollars and cents. The unethical operation, unless it is run by the Mafia or some other Big Baddie, is doomed to failure.

15. *Getting canned.* If it's important enough, hang on to your conviction and be willing to be fired over it.

16. *Job appointments.* Keep your buddies out of the joint unless they have survived competitive recruitment and can do the work better than anyone else. Most employees take their jobs seriously and resent hacks telling them how to run their shop.

17. *Laws (explicit).* Obey them until they are changed.

18. *Laws (unclear).* Seek a legal opinion or formal interpretation before you act! It can be worth the short time it takes to go through the procedure.

19. *Office supplies.* Keep your hands off them for personal use. Yes, that includes stamps and envelopes! By the way, have you stopped using your office budget to pay for long-distance telephone calls to the family?

20. *Passing the buck.* It's easy to do, considering the bureaucratic red tape often set up in most organizations which immobilizes decision making and action. But if a decision is within your realm of authority, make it; quit shrinking from the possibility of criticism. It can be exciting and a real test of your leadership ability to defend your choice.

21. *Performance.* If you can't see it, hear it, touch it, or measure it, you aren't performing. Somewhere along the line, you have to be measured according to agreed-upon standards or targets. If you cannot be, expect the axe. (While you're at it, don't forget to strive for excellence.)

22. *Preparation.* Prepare meticulously for important events and presentations. Demand the same from your staff.

23. *Quality.* Demand that your standards for quality performance be met. When they are not, let the recalcitrants and laggards *know* that their performance is unacceptable.

24. *Red tape.* Be a crusader against red tape, but not against the accountability which may have been the reason for instituting the sticky stuff.

Standards and Values

25. *Special interest groups.* Everyone runs into them at one time or another. Realize the consequences of going for or against one of these groups. Also recognize that there may be several others you should consider contacting for a balanced view on issues. Invite groups to air their ideas or protests, but don't forget the weight of decisions related to their concerns are still on *your* shoulders.

26. *Surprises.** Keep them to a minimum. Don't hand them out; don't accept them.

* Negative, harmful, counterproductive surprises that threaten to take control of a situation or cause a disruption. Not to include positive surprises—birthdays, new products, and other happy things.

27. Maxims to Operate and Succeed By

May the good Lord take a liking to you because not everyone will—*or* Even my mother didn't like me all the time, but she let me come home anyway.

It's a little silly to think a manager cannot survive if heavenly choirs fail to descend singing hymns of praise on a regular basis.

In the words of corporate chairman and chief executive officer James F. Beré, "Perhaps the hardest lesson to learn . . . is *don't try to be universally loved or admired.* If that's your goal, you'll fail. You don't have to seek approval; it will come if it's deserved."*

Someone is bound not to like you. Perhaps several someones.

* *Passages Magazine,* vol. 8, no. 3, June 1977. James F. Beré is with the Borg-Warner Corporation in Chicago.

The secret of survival is to admit it and not to fight it. You have to nowadays, because it no longer is possible to behead everyone who insults the queen.

Don't wear spurs in a paper airplane.

If you face a delicate situation, don't go into it wearing your spurs or you'll rip it apart. Instead, dress for the occasion. Cloak yourself in diplomacy. Vest yourself with wisdom, and wear a smile.

Don't spit into the wind—*or* Mud thrown is ground lost.*

Consider very carefully what might happen if you throw mud at the disagreeable people with whom you have to work. It's a temptation, to be sure. But remember, what goes around comes around. It is an idiot who does not realize that those muddied will surely be met again as potholes in the road to success.

Don't kiss a frog if he's your brother.

There are some people who should not be allowed to die until they finish what they've started on earth. Famous anthropologist Margaret Mead was one of them. Shortly before her death, she published an article in which she called for a universal awakening of the need to establish sex taboos in the working world. Well, she gave us the proposal. Is there anyone else as capable to carry it to the next step of action? Maybe it's you! Read on and see what you think.

What should we—what can we—do about sexual harassment on the job? Mead begins, "But who among us hasn't met the male kiss-and-tell office flirt, the pinching prankster, the man in search of party girls, or the man who makes sex a condition of job promotion?"*

Plenty of women would back you up on that one, Dr. Mead.

* An Adlai Stevenson quote.
* Margaret Mead, "A Proposal: We Need Taboos on Sex at Work," *Redbook Magazine,* vol. 130, no. 6, April 1978.

One executive described the sexual harassment she received from a male associate with whom she had to work closely. "I wanted him to look at me as if I were his best fishing partner. He wanted to look at me as if I were his bed partner for the night . . . It's intimidating. It's also repulsive if the come-ons happen too many times."

Another explained it this way. "When a woman is the boss back home in her own territory, a man is likely to listen and do as she requests. Or at least offer her his support or reject her ideas in all due respect. But put a woman at an out-of-town meeting or national convention where men are not quite certain as to her authority, capabilities, values, or mode of operation and she becomes the target of ye old girlfriend/boyfriend ritual laced in cajolery. Somehow, male/female *business* relationships are nonexistent or totally ignored, unless she gets downright frank with the man. It's degrading and embarrassing. It makes a woman wonder who's in control."

And still another pointed out the awkward situation many face because society has not fully recognized that men and women can have a strictly business relationship. "I don't want my husband, whom I love very much, to ever worry about what I'm up to. But I can't guarantee that as long as his friends see me in a restaurant with a male client and assume I must be having an affair. Can any spouse be so trusting as to *always* believe in his wife when best friends say otherwise? Well, I won't quit my job over it. But it sure would make it a lot easier if people understood."

For years magazines have told young women how to play the singles dating game. Until recently, very few have addressed the female/male work situation, where motives for relating are different. Writers, many of them, are now exploring these relationships. Still, no one has done so as well as Margaret Mead.

"A taboo enjoins. We need one that says clearly and unequivocally, 'You don't make passes at or sleep with the people you work with.'" She suggests that such a taboo can be likened to the one on incest which insures that "most children can grow up safe in the household, learn to trust, to be loved, and to be

sexually safe, unexploited and unmolested within the family.
. . . Like the family, the modern business and the modern
profession must develop incest taboos . . . [if we are to establish]
new ways that allow women and men to work together effort-
lessly and to respect each other as persons."*

Margaret Mead's proposal was meant to protect meaningful
human relationships, not destroy them. As one female executive
rephrased it in her own beliefs, "It's not that I want to erase the
love/sex relationship; I just don't want it at work!"

So until the area of business is made "safe," develop the skill
of tactfully dealing with sexual harassment on the job, pray that
it works, and say loudly and clearly, "I don't want to kiss you;
you're my brother."

If it ain't broke, don't fix it.

If things are working well, don't change them. You already
know this, you say? Perhaps you do, academically, but do you
practice it? This basic maxim is one of the most difficult to live
by, because fixing is such fun.

But remember, old production methods do not necessarily
mean inefficient methods. Unpopular bosses are not necessarily
poor bosses—perhaps they are doing a terrific job of managing
and should be allowed to continue in spite of staff grumbling.
And, because a group of people would rather change things
does not necessarily mean their changes would be better than
the present mode of operation.

It is an efficient and effective manager who spends her valuable time on fixing and not tinkering.

Don't drop your tree in an empty forest.

It's great to hold fine convictions. It's grand to stand on principle. But if convictions and principles are kept quiet or shared
with an empty world, they may not be worth much. There are
times, even when the woods are full of snipers, when you've got

* Margaret Mead, same article.

to drop the tree so that others can hear it. And even if you're the only one with the courage to swing the axe.

Here is an example: A young, midlevel manager we know challenged the chief executive officer (CEO) of one of the nation's largest corporations, in a forest filled with snipers. As a result, she helped change the landscape and disarmed the snipers.

It happened when our manager friend attended a dinner for the CEO (who later went on to become a member of the President's Cabinet). When she arrived on the scene, eager for her first glimpse of the prestigious, powerful big boss, she was dismayed to find that other company women present were mainly secretaries, there to help the men put on their plastic, pocket-type name tags. (They didn't know quite what to do with the female executive because she had no convenient pocket on her dress.)

The boss gave an impressive address, including remarks about new equal employment opportunities for women. He said he was pleased to see women in the large audience of executives. At the conclusion of his speech he called for questions. Several of the men rose and asked questions and the speaker answered them. Meanwhile, in the back of the room, our manager was steaming. She had put up with a lot of sexist teasing since coming to the corporation; nowhere had she seen any evidence of a real commitment to equal opportunity for women in management. She weighed the obvious risks, then got to her feet.

Among her questions were, Did the CEO *really* know what was going on in this division of the corporation? Did he have *any* idea of the way female managers were treated by the men, including those present in the room? And how did he intend to *see* that these new directions and approaches were implemented?

Some of the men began to laugh at her; others applauded— "It wasn't what I was saying," she told us, "they were applauding my bravado." But the CEO took her seriously. At first, the managers and the men around her assumed she would be expelled from the corporate forest. However, it was evident that she would not be when the CEO encouraged her comments and questions. It was further evident when he invited her, from the podium, to come to corporate headquarters to advise him on how best to make changes. Which is precisely what she did.

The story has a very positive ending. And it took one courageous woman, willing to risk her job for her convictions, and one CEO who was willing to listen.

Don't badmouth your enemies. Just remember who they are.*

Enough said.

Would I lie to you? I'm your mother!

A good mother is able to build trust and be the leader if she is able to demonstrate to her children that *their* interests and welfare are foremost in her mind, whatever action she takes.

No liar's poker for her. She says what she means and means what she says.

As a good mom, she also plays with her cards on top of the table, but never feels forced to turn them all face up until she is ready to make her move. Her kids learn to play better because of her style. But let her misdeal and she forfeits her chance to make a positive impact on family behavior and goals.

There's not much difference between kids and employees, except one thing. When disgusted, good employees can pack up and leave, *never* to return. Kids have a little more trouble doing that.

Don't put paint on a rotten board.

A new title will not make an ineffective program work. A new gimmick will not save (for long) a poor product. There are some things (or people) that just have to be replaced.

* A quote, of sorts, from Joe Kennedy.

Crow has better flavor when eaten voluntarily.

Q. *How do I know when to eat crow?*
A. When you are *dead wrong* and should be the first to admit it.
Q. *How should I eat it?*
A. With GRACE . . . or Richard or Virginia or Bob or whoever deserves the honor.

Doctors who smile get fewer lawsuits.

It is difficult to remain angry at someone who is kind and fair even when she must perform a little corrective surgery.

28. What's Next?

Do NOT look for any of the following in these pages:

- Six sure steps to that one great job.
- Ten ways to succeed in management.
- How to get to the top of the ladder by following the right mentor.

Life in the working world is not that simple and not that organized. Having said that, we will insist that there *are* things you can do to improve your chances of success, and we've already discussed many of them in this book. There are basics one *must* have to make it to the top, but you must understand that having them does not ensure entrance to the executive lunchroom.

We believe that there are some critical factors to success: knowing whether or not you have the necessary tools for management, knowing how to get those tools if you do not have them, knowing as much as possible about organizational life and your opportunities within it, and being able to make realistic career decisions.

In the long run, whom you know may be important, what you know certainly will be important, but the key will be how well you know yourself and what you really can do, want to do, and where you want to do it. And that is why we have presented the information in this book the way we have—to help you increase your understanding of your own managerial abilities and interest.

This understanding should help you make the important career decisions that come along. Realize that there will be many such decisions—it is rarely a woman-finds-great-job, woman-falls-in-love-with-job, woman-stays-in-great-job-forever kind of world. We must make important career decisions again and again. Even women who have been happy and secure in terrific jobs of long standing tell us that they frequently are faced with tough career choices. If this book has done nothing else, we sincerely hope that it has helped you realize the need to make many decisions about your job and yourself and that it has provided you with insight about both *you* and *management* that will help you make those decisions.

For our part, we are forever making decisions. To leave teaching or not? To become a government administrator or not? To move from a newspaper editorship to something different in spite of increasing national recognition for our work? To go into freelance work to have more flexibility when raising a family? And what happens when a terrific job turns into a health-destroying monster? How about private corporate life—is it the right way to go? Perhaps a business of one's own is the answer. And are we certain we really like the role of managing organizations for the rest of our lives?

And, of course, we've faced many more decisions—in spite of some fairly well-established career goals and directions. It is just

252

that one cannot always plan everything. Opportunity rarely sends advance notice of its arrival. Therefore, while we strongly advocate careful and thoughtful career planning and replanning, we believe that the key lies in the ability to make the right decisions whenever and wherever they must be made.

Finally, people who are extraordinarily successful often talk about "finding a need and filling it." This usually brings to mind a product—Orville Redenbacher and his fully popped popcorn, for example. But it can work the same way with a service or a job. Once you *really* know your talents, abilities, and interests, you may well be able to identify a new and more significant role for yourself in your present organization or in a different organization that needs what you can offer (whether or not they know it before you approach them). Or you may identify a job you would like to have but for which you lack a requisite skill, perhaps money management. In this case, you can move quickly to pick up that skill and then go after the job. The need you find may even offer you a chance to go on your own and start an entirely new business. The point is this: Do not sit and wait for the decision-making opportunities to come to you. Create them.

What's next for you? Name it. And go after it. While you are doing that, we will decide what to do next. One of us finally got the courage to leave that monster job for more comfortable pastures which may or may not be as green, and the other created an entirely new work pattern consisting of several jobs so that she had more time to spend with her husband and two small children. Once again, we find ourselves making important new career decisions. And they will not be our last!

Index

255

INDEX

INDEX

INDEX

INDEX

265

INDEX

Static, 63
Status quo, vs. change, 247
Stereotyping, as turnoff, 84–85
Stevenson, Adlai, 245n.
Strategic planning, neglecting, 122
Strategy, neglecting, 122
Student Nonviolent Coordinating Committee, 208
Studio costs, for teleconferencing, 176
Style (leadership), choosing, 29–30
Subordinates, 99
  countering male putdowns, 93
  functions of, 44–45
  pressures, 21
  see also Staff
Success
  maxims for, 244–250
  power as key, 89
  and self-confidence, 89–90
Supervision, 23
  of computer systems, 188
Supplies, office, 242
Support, vs. endorsement, 203
Supportive listening, 53, 57, 165
Surprises, negative and positive, 243n.
Survival, secrets of, 244–245

Taboos (sex), need for, 245–247
Tactics, for small-group meetings, 164–165
Task force, 193–197
  budgeting, 195
  controls for, 194
  death date, 196
  forming, 194
  selecting members, limiting authority, 195–196
  tactical tool, 196–197
  work activities, 194–195
Teamwork, and delegation, 206

Technical/functional competence, as career anchor, 228
Teleconferencing, 175–179
  costs, 176–177
Telephone-line costs, for teleconferencing, 176
Telephoning, contributors to small-group meetings, 158
Television cable companies, and teleconferencing, 179
Tension reduction, at small-group meetings, 162–163
Tergiversating, 56, 63
Terminals, of computers, 185
Terminology, computer, 185
Theory vs. practice, in planning, 123–124
Thruput, 94n.
Time, and computer systems, 185n.–186n.
Tinkering, vs. fixing, 247
Tipping, 111
Tokenism, in management, 76–78
Topics, for creative conferences, 168
Tracy, Diane, 177n.
Transmission costs, for teleconferencing, 176
Transmitting, 61, 63
Travel, 101–102, 103
  and newborn baby, 238
Travel funds, 98, 108
Trust, 31, 249
  and paranoia, 21–22
"Turkey farming," 40–42
Two-way communication, 63

Unauthorized activities, and computers, 190
Understanding
  and listening, 54
  and male putdowns, 93

Ann Thompson

ANN McKAY THOMPSON, one of 10 Outstanding Young Women in America in 1973, has an unusual career background in management, communications, small business, and education.

After completing a 1977 Bush Summer Fellow for Management Studies at MIT, Ann was appointed by the governor of South Dakota to serve in his cabinet and head the Department of Labor. Prior to that she held executive positions in the South Dakota Department of Education and Cultural Affairs and as the head of the Governor's Commission on the Status of Women.

Ann's long-time involvement with family businesses, management, and theater provided her with special skills in conducting successful seminars and conferences on management strategies and upward mobility for women.

Ann, a former teacher of writing and research, and former editor of a major educational bulletin, lives in South Dakota with her husband, attorney Charles M. Thompson, and their two small children, Murray and McLean. With partner, Marcia Wood, Ann is now presenting executive seminars around the country.

Marcia Wood

AWARD-WINNING journalist Marcia Donnan Wood has success-fully combined careers in communications and management. After receiving top national presswoman honors for 1972, Mar-cia joined state government, a career change that culminated with her appointment as South Dakota's first female cabinet of-ficer. Later, she became director of human resources devel-opment for the Corporation for Public Broadcasting in Washington, D.C., a role that focused on both management and communications. She recently has launched her own communi-cations management firm and is creating television projects. She has served in senior management positions; has designed and conducted employee and management development programs, seminars, and workshops; and has spoken on college campuses about women at work. She serves on the National Board of Directors of the Women's Equity Action League (WEAL). Mar-cia is married to U.S. Labor Department executive Charles A. Wood, Jr., and has a son, Alan, and a daughter, Kristin. This is her third book. She published *Cosmetics from the Kitchen* in 1972 and *Raindance to Research* in 1977.